# Practicing for Today's Tests

Level **6** Language Arts

**Author**
Suzanne Barchers

## Introduction Author

Delia E. Racines, Ph.D.
Faculty, University of Southern California
USC Language Academy

## Publishing Credits

Corinne Burton, M.A.Ed., *President*; Emily R. Smith, M.A.Ed., *Editorial Director*; Debra J. Housel, M.S.Ed., *Editor*; Jennifer Wilson, *Editor*; Courtney Patterson, *Multimedia Designer*; Stephanie Bernard, *Assistant Editor*; Monique Dominquez, *Production Artist*

## Image Credits

p. 72, 78: iStock; All other images from Shutterstock unless noted otherwise.

## Standards

© Copyright 2010. National Governors Association Center for Best Practices and Council of Chief State School Officers. All rights reserved.

### Shell Education

5301 Oceanus Drive
Huntington Beach, CA 92649-1030
http://www.shelleducation.com
**ISBN 978-1-4258-1439-7**
© 2015 Shell Educational Publishing, Inc.

# Table of Contents

# Today's Next Generation Tests

"To be college and career ready, students must now read across a broad range of high-quality texts from diverse cultures and times in history."

—Delia E. Racines, Ph.D.

Education is currently undergoing a dramatic shift when it comes to the ways we measure and assess for learning. Educational standards across the nation are designed to provide clear and meaningful goals for our students. These standards serve as a frame of reference for educators, parents, and students and are most critical when decisions must be made about curriculum, textbooks, assessments, and other aspects of instructional programs (Conley 2014). Part of the disconnect with standards in the recent past has been the vast differences and lack of consistency in expectations that became a major concern for the quality of education students were receiving across the country (Conley 2014; Wiley and Wright 2004).

Standards in education in the United States are not a new concept. However, the role of educational standards has recently shifted to not only ensure that all students have access to equitable education no matter where they live, but also to ensure a more consistent national expectation for what all students should know to be successful in a rapidly changing economy and society (Kornhaber, Griffith, and Tyler 2014).

Scales, scores, and assessments are absolutely necessary to ascertain the current status of students. This kind of data is vital for teachers to understand what is missing and what the next steps should be. The real question about assessment isn't whether we should assess but rather what kinds of assessments should be used. Along with the current shift to more consistent and rigorous standards, states now measure student progress with assessments that require higher-order thinking skills necessary for preparation for college and/or careers.

So, what is this new yardstick that is being used? How is it better than yardsticks of the past? And how do we best prepare students to be measured with this yardstick in a way that tells the whole story? The next generation tests intend to provide results that are comparable across all states and will use more performance-based tasks as well as technology-enhanced items. This is very different in comparison to the standardized testing that teachers, students, and parents are used to (National Governors Association Center for Best Practices 2010; Rothman 2013).

The following descriptions serve as explanations of how the three most prominent next-generation tests are different from assessments of the past.

# Today's Next Generation Tests *(cont.)*

## Partnership for Assessment of Readiness for College and Careers (PARCC)

The PARCC assessment is a common set of computer-based, K–12 assessments in English language arts and mathematics. These assessments replace previous state tests in grades 3–11 used to meet the requirements of the Elementary and Secondary Education Act (PARCC 2013). The most significant difference in the PARCC tests is the use of performance tasks that ask students to apply their knowledge to solve extended problems rather than simply regurgitate answers (Rothman 2013).

PARCC consists of four assessments a year. The two optional assessments include diagnostic assessments (in reading, writing, and mathematics) that may be administered at the beginning of each school year and as mid-year assessments to help predict students' likely end-of-year performances.

The two required summative assessments consist of a performance task and an end-of-year test for each grade. Previously, in English language arts, many states did not assess writing and few assessed critical-thinking skills. The PARCC assessment does both. The performance-based assessment is in English language arts and mathematics and includes asking students to analyze literature as well as narrative writing tasks. Students also take the end-of-year assessments in English language arts and mathematics. The results of the two tests are combined to determine the summative assessment score (PARCC 2013). Lastly, a separate speaking and listening component is required and can be administered anytime during the academic year. The results of the speaking and listening component are not be combined with the other assessments to determine students' summative assessment scores.

*Many of today's standardized tests are administered online.*

# Today's Next Generation Tests (cont.)

## Smarter Balanced Assessment Consortium (SBAC)

The SBAC is also developing summative assessments in English language arts and mathematics. Their assessments have two major components: performance tasks and an end-of-the-year computer adaptive test. Computer adaptive tests mean that questions are adjusted based on students' previous responses. These two major components are administered during the last 12 weeks of the school year (SBAC 2014). The computer adaptive test feature, which is the biggest difference from the PARCC, is intended to enable administrators and teachers to use results within weeks to more efficiently and quickly identify students' ability levels in an effort to differentiate instruction. The SBAC assessments go beyond multiple-choice tests to include short constructed responses, extended constructed responses, and performance tasks. These allow students to complete in-depth projects that demonstrate both analytical skills and real-world problem solving (SBAC 2014). Performance tasks are online in reading, writing, and mathematics and may also be administered as part of the optional interim assessments throughout the year. Results will be available within weeks after a student completes a performance task.

## State of Texas Assessment of Academic Readiness (STAAR®)

The STAAR® replaced the Texas Assessment of Knowledge and Skills (TAKS). It was developed and adopted by the Texas School Board of Education within the Texas Education Agency. This assessment focuses on readiness for college and/or careers with test questions that focus on rigor and critical analysis.

For elementary school and middle school, the tests cover the same subjects and grades as the previous state testing program, the TAKS. The most significant differences between the TAKS and the STAAR® are apparent at the high school level with 12 end-of-course assessments that focus on fewer skills in a deeper manner and replace previous grade-specific tests (Texas Education Agency 2014). The STAAR® assesses the Texas Essential Knowledge and Skills. However, there are a greater number of items with higher cognitive demands. In writing, students are required to write two essays instead of one.

# Categories of Questions

In order for students today to be better prepared for college and/or careers, they must be able to read widely and deeply across a range of informational and literary texts (National Governors Association Center for Best Practices 2010). In today's standards, there are often three categories of reading standards. On assessments, these categories are represented by three categories of questions. The questions include new terminology that defines specific skills and understandings that all students must demonstrate. **Note:** See *Appendix B* (pages 100–103) for how these categories are represented in each practice exercise in this book.

Overall, today's college and career readiness reading standards depict the picture of what students should be able to exhibit with increasing proficiency and on a regular basis. To be college and career ready, students must now read across a broad range of high-quality texts from diverse cultures and times in history. The reading standards emphasize the skills necessary to critically read and continuously make connections among ideas and texts. Students also learn to distinguish poor reasoning as well as ambiguities in texts. The following explanation of the terms related to each of the three reading categories will better prepare educators and parents for today's tests.

## Key Ideas and Details

This category stresses the importance of understanding specific information in various texts. Overall, students must be able to identify specific details and then gain deeper meaning from what is read. Specifically, this category requires students to be able to do the following things.

| Students should be able to . . . | To show how they know this, students must . . . |
|---|---|
| read text closely to really understand what it says. | identify specific details from the text. |
| make conclusions based on what they identify from a text. | say or write specific details to support their conclusions. |
| determine the main idea or theme from a text and analyze its development. | identify and summarize key supporting details that support the theme or main idea. |
| figure out how and why individuals, events, or ideas develop and interact over the course of a text. | explain details about how characters and/or the story develop at different times throughout the text from the beginning to the end. |

# Categories of Questions *(cont.)*

## Craft and Structure

This category stresses the importance of being able to identify patterns of various text structures to more easily synthesize and summarize information. Physical text structures (captions, pictures, diagrams, italicized print, bold print, etc.) are purposely used in texts to organize different types of information. This is true for both fiction and nonfiction texts. Specifically, this category requires students to be able to do the following things.

| Students should be able to . . . | To show how they know this, students must . . . |
| --- | --- |
| interpret words and phrases as they are used in technical, connotative, or figurative texts. | explain the purposes of different types of texts and distinguish what kinds of words or phrases are used in each type. |
| analyze how specific word choices shape meaning or tone. | identify and explain why certain words are used and how different words alter the feelings readers experience from texts. |
| analyze the parts or structures of a text. | identify the names and purposes of each different structure within a text. |
| explain the relationships between parts or structures within a text. | explain how sentences, paragraphs, and larger portions of texts relate to one another and the whole text. |
| figure out how point of view shapes the content and style of a text. | explain how different perspectives could change the meaning of a text. |
| figure out how purpose changes the content and style of a text. | explain how different purposes could alter the meaning of a text. |

# Categories of Questions *(cont.)*

## Integration of Knowledge and Ideas

This category stresses the importance of being able to understand the main idea of texts and analyze details presented in various formats. Students should then be able to draw conclusions based on the text, interpret the purpose and structure of texts, and apply the meaning across other texts and knowledge. In general, students should compare and contrast texts and ultimately increase comprehensibility of more complex texts. Specifically, this category requires students to be able to do the following things.

| Students should be able to . . . | To show how they know this, students must . . . |
|---|---|
| evaluate content presented in various formats (e.g., in writing, visually, via media, and numerically). | describe what they understand about the content through various formats. |
| integrate or put together cross-curricular content that is presented in different formats. | explain how ideas presented in various formats are related to one another. |
| outline what the argument is in a text. | identify specific claims in a text that include how valid the reasoning is in the argument, how relevant the reasoning is to the argument, and whether there is enough evidence to support the argument. |
| analyze how two or more texts address similar themes or topics to build knowledge or to compare the approaches the authors take. | identify themes of multiple texts and then describe similarities and differences between the texts. |
| compare the approaches different authors take. | identify the approaches different authors take and then describe similarities and differences between them. |

# Making It Meaningful

The section has been included to make this book's test practice more meaningful. The purpose of this section is to provide sample guiding questions framed around a specific practice exercise. This will serve as a meaningful and real-life application of the test practice. Each of the guiding questions serves as a thinking prompt to ensure that the three categories of the reading standards have been considered. The guiding questions may be used with students as a teacher-led think aloud or to individually assess how students are approaching and understanding complex texts. The framework used in this model serves as a template for how to approach other fiction and nonfiction texts. The template supports educators in preparing students for today's tests and helps make meaning of the reading standards to ultimately ensure that the learning becomes more meaningful for all students.

**Begin with the Craft and Structure reading standards in mind by asking students these questions:**

What type of text is this?

What is the purpose of this type of text?

Identify what text structures are used in this text and why.

What is the relationship among certain vocabulary words?

How do the words shape the tone?

**Then, with the Key Ideas and Details reading standards in mind, coach students to do the following:**

Underline the key details you have noticed so far.

Write a summary sentence with these details as support.

List or create a timeline of important events in the character's story.

**Finally, check for understanding with the Integration of Knowledge and Ideas reading standards in mind by asking students to do the following:**

Make connections across other content areas.

Explain how varied ideas relate to one another.

# Making It Meaningful *(cont.)*

Sometimes, students will be asked questions about graphics or captions.

"Illustrations, pictures, graphics, and captions are types of text structures. What is the purpose of the specific text structure in this text?"

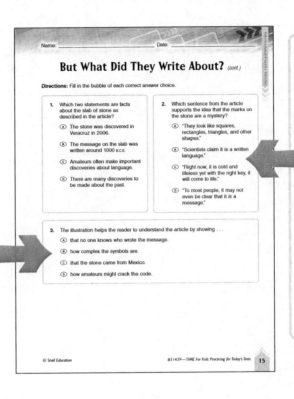

When questions refer to specific sentences, guide the students in the following way:

"This question references a specific sentence in the text. Go back and **highlight** or <u>underline</u> this sentence. Then, reread the text around that sentence to find the answer the question."

When students are asked vocabulary questions, help them in the following way:

"Find the specific vocabulary word in the text and circle it. Use the other words around it to figure out its meaning using context clues."

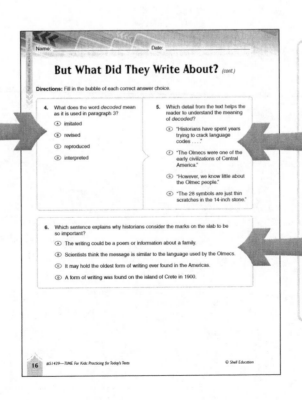

For all questions, students should do the following:

"Ask yourself what the directions are asking you to do. Do you need to analyze, infer, evaluate, formulate, describe, support, explain, summarize, compare, contrast, predict, fill in, complete, etc.?"

# Making It Meaningful *(cont.)*

If students need to complete graphic organizers, use guiding questions to help them determine how the text can help them respond.

"Where in the text does it discuss what is known and what is not known about the Mexican Stone? Reread the text to locate and write the phrases that can complete the chart."

Name: _____  Date: _____

## But What Did They Write About? *(cont.)*

**Directions:** Answer the questions.

7. Complete the chart below. Write four phrases or sentences from the text in each column.

| What is KNOWN about the Mexican stone? | What is NOT KNOWN about the Mexican stone? |
|---|---|
| | |
| | |
| | |
| | |

8. How does the find from 1900 relate to the Mexican stone?

_____
_____
_____
_____

© Shell Education      #51439—TIME For Kids: Practicing for Today's Tests      **17**

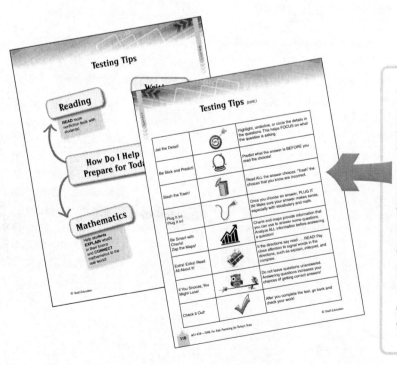

To support students in preparing for today's tests, send home the Testing Tips flyers on pages 109–110. There is one page intended to guide parents in how to prepare their children and a second page to help students understand ways they can be more succssful while taking tests.

Name: _____    Date: _____

# But What Did They Write About?

**Directions:** Read this text and respond to the questions on pages 15–17.

1 A slab of stone in Mexico holds a message. We do not know what that message is, and we may never know. We do not know who wrote it or even know what language it is written in. It was written over 3,000 years ago, around 1000 B.C.E. It was discovered in the Mexican state of Veracruz in 2006.

2 To most people, it may not even be clear that it *is* a message. The 28 symbols are just thin scratches in the 14-inch (35-cm) stone. They look like squares, rectangles, triangles, and other shapes. Yet scientists are sure it is a written message in a language similar to the one used by the Olmecs. The Olmecs were one of the early civilizations of Central America. Some of their buildings still stand, along with massive carved stone heads. However, we know little about the Olmec people.

3 Scientists claim it is a written language. If they are right, that small stone may hold the oldest form of writing ever found in the Americas. But we may never know what it says. A form of writing was found on the island of Crete in the Mediterranean Sea in 1900, yet after more than a century of trying, nobody has decoded it.

*Look closely at the message carved in this stone slab.*

Michael D. Coe

# But What Did They Write About? *(cont.)*

4  It is hard to imagine what the Olmecs could have written down. Is it a list of items owned by a wealthy merchant? Is it somebody's family tree? Could it be a poem— and if so, about what?

5  That small piece of stone is like a locked time machine. Right now, it is cold and lifeless yet with the right key, it will come to life. We will try to decode it, and if we succeed, it will speak to us in the voice of people who have been gone for 3,000 years. We do not even know what language it would speak; we just know that it would be fascinating.

6  Historians have spent years trying to crack language codes, and the Mexican stone "time machine" shows that there are still many discoveries to be made.

This stone slab was found in 2006.

Michael D. Coe

Name: _____ Date: _____

# But What Did They Write About? *(cont.)*

**Directions:** Fill in the bubble of each correct answer choice.

1. Which two statements are facts about the slab of stone as described in the article?

   Ⓐ The stone was discovered in Veracruz in 2006.

   Ⓑ The message on the slab was written around 1000 B.C.E.

   Ⓒ Amateurs often make important discoveries about language.

   Ⓓ There are many discoveries to be made about the past.

2. Which sentence from the article supports the idea that the marks on the stone are a mystery?

   Ⓐ "They look like squares, rectangles, triangles, and other shapes."

   Ⓑ "Scientists claim it is a written language."

   Ⓒ "Right now, it is cold and lifeless yet with the right key, it will come to life."

   Ⓓ "To most people, it may not even be clear that it *is* a message."

3. The illustration helps the reader to understand the article by showing . . .

   Ⓐ that no one knows who wrote the message.

   Ⓑ how complex the symbols are.

   Ⓒ that the stone came from Mexico.

   Ⓓ how amateurs might crack the code.

Name: _____ Date: _____

# But What Did They Write About? *(cont.)*

**Directions:** Fill in the bubble of each correct answer choice.

4. What does the word *decoded* mean as it is used in paragraph 3?

   Ⓐ imitated

   Ⓑ revised

   Ⓒ reproduced

   Ⓓ interpreted

5. Which detail from the text helps the reader to understand the meaning of *decoded*?

   Ⓔ "Historians have spent years trying to crack language codes . . . ."

   Ⓕ "The Olmecs were one of the early civilizations of Central America."

   Ⓖ "However, we know little about the Olmec people."

   Ⓗ "The 28 symbols are just thin scratches in the 14-inch stone."

6. Which sentence explains why historians consider the marks on the slab to be so important?

   Ⓐ The writing could be a poem or information about a family.

   Ⓑ Scientists think the message is similar to the language used by the Olmecs.

   Ⓒ It may hold the oldest form of writing ever found in the Americas.

   Ⓓ A form of writing was found on the island of Crete in 1900.

Name: _____     Date: _____

# But What Did They Write About? *(cont.)*

**Directions:** Answer the questions.

7. Complete the chart below. Write four phrases or sentences from the text in each column.

| What is KNOWN about the Mexican stone? | What is NOT KNOWN about the Mexican stone? |
|---|---|
|  |  |
|  |  |
|  |  |
|  |  |

8. How does the find from 1900 relate to the Mexican stone?

_____

_____

_____

_____

Name: _____  Date: _____

# Peggy Whitson's Long Road to Space

**Directions:** Read this text and respond to the questions on pages 20–22.

1   Dr. Peggy Whitson is a biochemist who has lived in outer space. In 2002, she became the first scientist to live at the International Space Station. She lived there for six months, orbiting Earth at 17,500 miles (28,163 km) per hour. She did experiments, slept in a floating sleeping bag, and drank liquids in zero gravity. She was living her dream.

2   It was a dream that began in 1969. Whitson was nine years old. She was living on a farm in Iowa when she watched the TV broadcast that showed Neil Armstrong and Buzz Aldrin become the first people to walk on the moon. She decided to become an astronaut, too. Later, when Whitson was in high school, NASA sent the first U.S. women into space. Sally Ride and Shannon Lucid were two of them. Lucid was a biochemist and an astronaut. Whitson wanted to be an astronaut scientist, like Lucid.

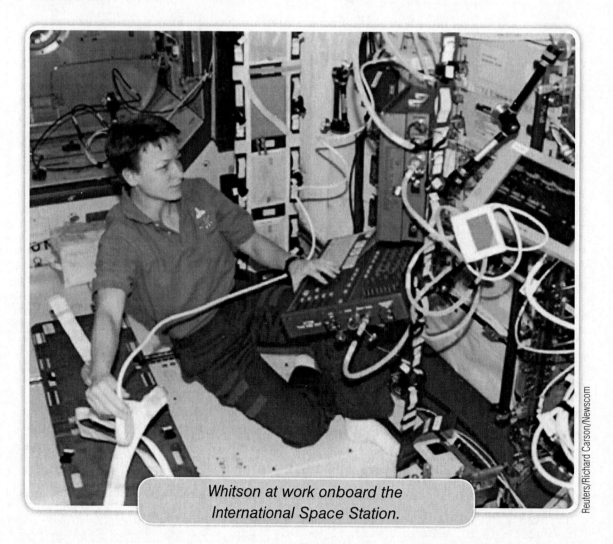

*Whitson at work onboard the International Space Station.*

Reuters/Richard Carson/Newscom

# Peggy Whitson's Long Road to Space *(cont.)*

3  Whitson was not always encouraged to pursue her dream. In college she studied biology and chemistry. Her teachers encouraged her to go to medical school. Whitson had other ideas.

4  "In my usual way, I did not pay any attention," she says. "I still wanted to be an astronaut."

5  Whitson graduated from college and went to Rice University in Houston, Texas, to do research. By coincidence, the school was next door to NASA's Johnson Space Center. In 1986, Whitson got closer to her goal. She got a job at the Space Center. She was not an astronaut yet, but she was working on the space program.

6  Once a year, Whitson applied for the astronaut training program. And once a year, she was turned down. In 1996, she was admitted! It was her tenth try. Peggy Whitson became an astronaut. She trained for six years before her first stay at the International Space Station. One of the experiments she did in space brought her back to her Iowan roots. She grew soybeans. She wanted to see how low gravity would affect them. She wanted to know if astronauts could grow plants on long trips to other planets.

7  Was her time in space worth the years of hard work? Yes. "Leaving the Space Station was extremely difficult," she says. Whitson went back to the International Space Station in 2007 and became the first female chief of NASA's Astronaut Office in 2009.

*The International Space Station*

# Peggy Whitson's Long Road to Space *(cont.)*

**Directions:** Fill in the bubble of each correct answer choice.

1. Which events inspired Peggy Whitson to become an astronaut? Choose all that apply.

   Ⓐ Whitson grew up on a farm in Iowa in the 1960s.

   Ⓑ She saw the TV broadcast of Neil Armstrong and Buzz Aldrin on the moon.

   Ⓒ NASA sent two women into space when Whitson was in high school.

   Ⓓ Whitson's teachers encouraged her to become an astronaut.

2. What does the author want the reader to infer from this sentence: "In my usual way, I did not pay any attention."

   Ⓐ Whitson found her dream when she was just a child.

   Ⓑ Whitson was inspired by Sally Ride and Shannon Lucid.

   Ⓒ Whitson decided that research was a good job.

   Ⓓ Whitson chose to keep pursuing her dream despite others' opinions.

3. Which statement from the article shows that Whitson has patience?

   Ⓐ "In 1996, she was admitted! It was her tenth try."

   Ⓑ "In college, she studied biology and chemistry."

   Ⓒ "Whitson wanted to be an astronaut scientist, too."

   Ⓓ "She got a job at the Space Center."

Name: _____  Date: _____

# Peggy Whitson's Long Road to Space *(cont.)*

**Directions:** Fill in the bubble of each correct answer choice.

**4.** What does the word *coincidence* mean as it is used in paragraph 5?

- Ⓐ plan
- Ⓑ chance
- Ⓒ arrangement
- Ⓓ agreement

**5.** Which statement from the article helps the reader to understand the importance of the word *coincidence*?

- Ⓔ Whitson wanted to be a scientist.
- Ⓕ Whitson did not pay any attention to some people.
- Ⓖ Whitson's college was near NASA's Johnson Space Center.
- Ⓗ Whitson really wanted to be an astronaut.

**6.** The photograph on page 18 shows Whitson at work aboard the International Space Station. What does the photograph help the reader to understand?

- Ⓐ It takes years of training to prepare for such a complicated job.
- Ⓑ Whitson was determined to become an astronaut.
- Ⓒ It could be useful to grow plants on long trips in space.
- Ⓓ Whitson found it difficult to leave the Space Station.

Name: _____ Date: _____

# Peggy Whitson's Long Road to Space *(cont.)*

**Directions:** Answer the questions.

7. Complete the time line with important events in Peggy Whitson's life. Write each event's year on one of the rectangular signposts.

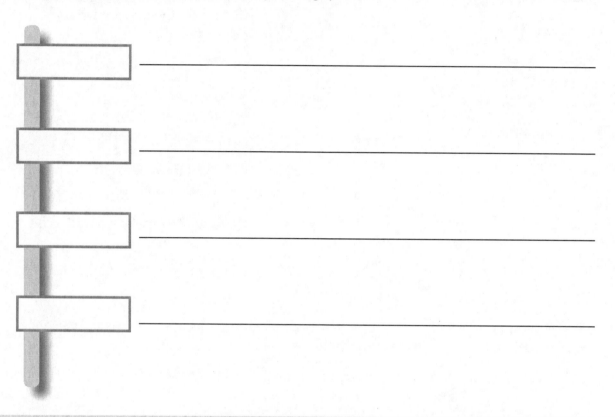

_____

_____

_____

_____

8. Answer this question from paragraph 7: "Was her time in space worth the years of hard work?" Use evidence from the text to explain your answer.

_____

_____

_____

_____

_____

Name: _____    Date: _____

# Science and the Environment: Are They Enemies?

**Directions:** Read this text and respond to the questions on pages 25–27.

1    Earth Day is celebrated every year on April 22 in schools and cities across the United States. There are class projects, programs, and tree plantings. There are many official events. But when it first started, Earth Day was seen as a radical protest.

2    The modern environmental movement began in the 1960s. It was a time when people were acting out against their parents' way of life. There were protests on college campuses. People were against the war in Vietnam and other issues. Gaylord Nelson, a U.S. Senator from Wisconsin, came up with the idea for Earth Day in 1970. He wanted to channel "the student antiwar energy into the environmental cause."

3    A lot of young people felt that science was the enemy even though some scientists were helpful. These scientists were warning the public about air and water pollution and animals in danger. Wasn't it technology—cars, housing developments, and factories—that was causing the problem? Wasn't it spreading pollution and destroying nature? Some adults thought Earth Day supporters had gone too far. These adults made fun of the supporters, calling them "tree huggers."

4    Environmentalists were right: Technology had to be controlled. Laws and regulations were needed. Industry and science both needed to act responsibly. Still, science got a bad name. It was as if you had to choose: science or nature. You couldn't have both.

*Science and nature can work together to keep the environment healthy.*

# Science and the Environment: Are They Enemies? *(cont.)*

5  Lately though, things have changed. People realize that science and the environment do not have to be enemies. Technology can be used to protect the environment. It does not have to hurt it.

6  Many clean energy ideas have come from science—including windmills and solar energy panels. These ideas reduce global climate change. Scientists have designed hybrid cars that can run on batteries or cheap fuel. Each of these can help cut down our use of fossil fuels such as oil, coal, and natural gas. None of these can be replaced. Scientists and engineers are working to invent earth-friendly fuels.

7  Earth Day has grown up, and so has our view of science and nature. Now we know that we do not have to choose between the two because science can be used to protect the environment. You can be a scientist and a tree hugger.

*Taking care of Earth is up to us.*

 #51439—TIME For Kids: Practicing for Today's Tests

# Science and the Environment: Are They Enemies? *(cont.)*

**Directions:** Fill in the bubble of each correct answer choice.

1.  Read this sentence from paragraph 2: "He wanted to channel 'the student antiwar energy into the environmental cause.'" Why does the author use quotation marks for part of this sentence?

    Ⓐ to show that the words are important details

    Ⓑ to show that the words come from a television show

    Ⓒ to show that the words come from Gaylord Nelson

    Ⓓ to show that the words are the main idea

2.  What does the word *radical* mean as it is used in paragraph 1?

    Ⓐ necessary

    Ⓑ extreme

    Ⓒ conservative

    Ⓓ basic

3.  Which sentence from the text best helps the reader to understand the meaning of *radical*?

    Ⓔ "It was a time when people were acting out against their parents' way of life."

    Ⓕ "The modern environmental movement began in the 1960s."

    Ⓖ "Gaylord Nelson, a U.S. Senator from Wisconsin, came up with the idea for Earth Day in 1970."

    Ⓗ "A lot of young people felt that science was the enemy even though some scientists were helpful."

Name: _____     Date: _____

# Science and the Environment: Are They Enemies? *(cont.)*

**Directions:** Fill in the bubble of each correct answer choice.

4.  Which two sentences from the article indicate that some people did not support Earth Day at first?

   (A) "Industry and science both needed to act responsibly."

   (B) "Some adults thought Earth Day supporters had gone too far."

   (C) "A lot of young people felt that science was the enemy even though some scientists were helpful."

   (D) "These adults made fun of the supporters, calling them 'tree huggers.'"

5.  Read this sentence from paragraph 6: "Scientists and engineers are working to invent earth-friendly fuels." What can you infer from this statement?

   (A) People are working together to solve fuel problems.

   (B) Scientists want to discover additional fossil fuels.

   (C) We cannot find new ways to cut down our use of fossil fuels.

   (D) Scientists need to find cheaper sources of fuel.

6.  Which statement is the best summary of the text?

   (A) Environmentalists in the 1960s and 1970s were right to worry about technology.

   (B) Hybrid cars, windmills, and solar energy are good ideas.

   (C) Businesses and science must both act responsibly.

   (D) Science can be used to help protect the environment.

Name: _____  Date: _____

# Science and the Environment: Are They Enemies? *(cont.)*

**Directions:** Answer the questions.

7.  Earth Day has changed a lot since the 1970s. Write four quotations from the text in each column to describe attitudes about Earth Day in the 1970s and now.

| Earth Day in the 1970s | Earth Day Now |
| --- | --- |
|  |  |

8.  Paragraph 7 states, "Earth Day has grown up, and so has our view of science and nature." Explain what you think is meant by this statement. Highlight information from the text to support your answer.

_____

_____

_____

_____

_____

Name: _____ Date: _____

# Dinos for Dinner

**Directions:** Read this text and respond to the questions on pages 30–32.

1  Even when dinosaurs ruled the earth, they sometimes ended up as a meal. Not just for other dinosaurs but also for mammals. Chinese and American paleontologists made this discovery. Paleontologists are scientists who study fossils. They were studying a fossil of a 130 million-year-old mammal called *Repenomamus robustus* (*R. robustus*). The scientists found the fossilized remains of its last meal— a baby dinosaur. The mammal had eaten a *psittacosaur*, a two-legged plant-eating dinosaur with a beaklike snout.

2  Farmers in China dug up this fossil in 2000. It was brought to researchers in Beijing, China. Then it was taken to the American Museum of Natural History in New York City. There researchers noticed a set of bones under its rib cage, where the mammal's stomach had likely been. The bones were the limbs, fingers, and teeth of a six-inch (15-cm) long *psittacosaur*.

3  Some of the eaten dinosaur's bones were joined. This suggests that it was swallowed in large, unchewed chunks. The rare fossil is the first sign that early mammals may have fed on young dinosaurs. "This discovery is the chance of a lifetime," Jin Meng says. He is a paleontologist at the American Museum of Natural History.

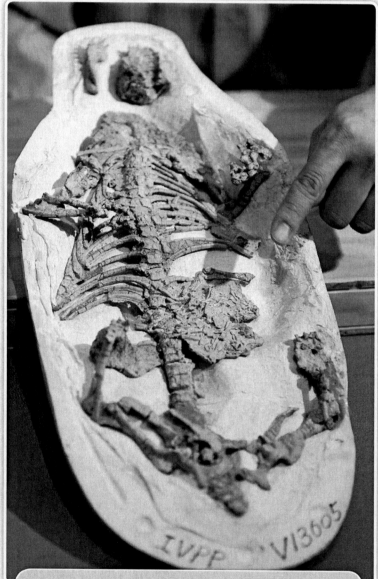

*A fossil of* Repenomamus robustus *with a bellyful of its last meal—a baby dinosaur*

AP Wide World

# Dinos for Dinner *(cont.)*

## Mammals Were Bigger, Too

4    Not only were mammals eating dinosaurs, the mammals were also bigger than previously thought. The team of scientists found another fossil in the same place in China in 2005. This animal was a bigger relative of *R. robustus*. It probably weighed about 30 pounds (13.6 kg). It is called *Repenomamus giganticus*. *R. robustus* was about 15 inches (38 cm) long. *R. giganticus* was twice that size. It is the largest known complete skeleton of a mammal from the Mesozoic era (280 million to 65 million years ago).

*The Mesozoic era was millions of years ago.*

5    Together, these two discoveries give scientists a new understanding of ancient mammals. Before these finds, experts thought that Mesozoic mammals were the size of squirrels and hunted mostly at night. These finds offer proof that some mammals were meat eaters who competed with small dinosaurs for food and territory.

6    Of course, 130 million years ago, most dinosaurs were larger, stronger, and moved faster than mammals. Still, these finds raise questions. How did these larger hunting mammals affect dinosaur evolution? The answer will have to wait for more evidence. "That's how it is with the best finds," says paleontologist Anne Weil of Duke University in North Carolina. "They leave you with more questions than answers."

# Dinos for Dinner (cont.)

**Directions:** Fill in the bubble of each correct answer choice.

1. What can you infer from the second paragraph? Choose all that apply.

   Ⓐ Farmers thought that the fossil might be important.

   Ⓑ Different scientists worked together to study the fossil.

   Ⓒ The *psittacosaur* dinosaur could not run very fast.

   Ⓓ The mammal was probably killed by a large dinosaur.

2. Which statement from the text suggests that paleontologists were excited about the fossil?

   Ⓐ "Chinese and American paleontologists made this discovery."

   Ⓑ "The scientists found the remains of its last meal—a baby dinosaur."

   Ⓒ "'This discovery is the chance of a lifetime,' Jin Meng says."

   Ⓓ "They leave you with more questions than answers."

3. What does the photograph of the dinosaur bones help the reader to understand?

   Ⓐ Experts thought Mesozoic mammals hunted at night.

   Ⓑ Some mammals competed with small dinosaurs for food.

   Ⓒ Farmers in China found an important fossil.

   Ⓓ The dinosaur bones were found in the mammal's stomach.

# Dinos for Dinner *(cont.)*

**Directions:** Fill in the bubble of each correct answer choice.

4. The article is mainly about how . . .

   Ⓐ a discovery changed scientists' thinking about mammals.

   Ⓑ meat-eating mammals competed with each other for food.

   Ⓒ researchers from different countries work with each other.

   Ⓓ scientists always have more questions than answers.

5. What does the word *ancient* mean as it is used in paragraph 5?

   Ⓐ antique

   Ⓑ tired

   Ⓒ prehistoric

   Ⓓ old-fashioned

6. Which of the sentences from the passage best helps the reader to understand the meaning of *ancient*?

   Ⓔ "These finds offer proof that some mammals were meat eaters who competed with small dinosaurs for food and territory."

   Ⓕ "Before these finds, experts thought that Mesozoic mammals were the size of squirrels and hunted mostly at night."

   Ⓖ "Not only were mammals eating dinosaurs, the mammals were also bigger than previously thought."

   Ⓗ "Of course 130 million years ago, most dinosaurs were larger, stronger, and moved faster than mammals."

Name: _____ Date: _____

# Dinos for Dinner *(cont.)*

**Directions:** Answer the questions.

7. Number these statements in the order in which the events happened.

   _____ Paleontologists found bones in the fossil's stomach.

   _____ Farmers in China dug up a fossil and sent it to Bejing.

   _____ Scientists discovered an animal called *Repenomamus giganticus*.

   _____ A mammal ate a baby dinosaur in large chunks.

   _____ Scientists realized that mammals were bigger than they thought.

8. Identify the main idea in the text's last paragraph. Use a quotation from the text in your response.

   _____

   _____

   _____

   _____

   _____

   _____

Name: _____  Date: _____

# A Royal Return to Russia

**Directions:** Read this text and respond to the questions on pages 35–37.

1  In 2004, Russia received an expensive gift. Victor Vekselberg, a businessman, brought a large collection back to his home country. The bounty included nine jeweled Fabergé Easter eggs. They had been made in the late 1800s for Russia's royal family. The family's surname was Romanov. The Romanovs were overthrown in 1918. Like much of the artwork made when the country was ruled by the royal family, the eggs were sold.

2  Vekselberg purchased the Fabergé eggs and other valuables in New York City. Together, the pieces are worth an estimated $100 million. Vekselberg bought a collection of eggs, jewelry, stone carvings, and gem-studded picture frames. He brought them to Russia. They are on display in a museum. "This was a once-in-a-lifetime chance to give back to my country one of its most revered treasures," he said. "I am honored to make this important collection available to the Russian public."

## Rich in History

3  Fabergé eggs have long been the symbolic crown jewel of Russia's royal past. They are named for Peter Carl Fabergé. He was the Russian jeweler who created them.

Michael D. Coe

*The flowers on this Lilies of the Valley egg are made of pearls and diamonds.*

# A Royal Return to Russia *(cont.)*

4   Fabergé created the first egg in 1885 for Czar Alexander III. The ruler had asked that the jeweler make an Easter gift for his wife. This started a tradition in the royal family that lasted more than 30 years.

5   Fabergé and his jewelers made a total of 50 eggs. The eggs were carefully crafted by hand. The Coronation Egg is made of gold enamel. It holds a tiny copy of the coach in which Czar Nicholas's queen rode into Moscow in 1896. It is the most valuable egg in Vekselberg's collection. The group also includes the Lilies of the Valley and Orange Tree eggs.

6   Russians celebrated the return of the treasures. "There has always been this dream," says Mikhail Piotrovsky. He is the director of the State Hermitage Museum in Saint Petersburg, Russia. "But I wasn't sure it would come true."

*The State Hermitage Museum*

# A Royal Return to Russia *(cont.)*

**Directions:** Fill in the bubble of each correct answer choice.

1. What can you conclude about Czar Alexander III from the article?

    Ⓐ He was beloved.

    Ⓑ He was clever.

    Ⓒ He was humble.

    Ⓓ He was wealthy.

2. What does the word *revered* mean as it is used in paragraph 2?

    Ⓐ valued

    Ⓑ disliked

    Ⓒ expected

    Ⓓ recognized

3. Which of the sentences from the passage best helps the reader to understand the meaning of *revered*?

    Ⓔ "It is the most valuable egg in Vekselberg's collection."

    Ⓕ "Fabergé and his jewelers made a total of 50 eggs."

    Ⓖ "The eggs were carefully crafted by hand."

    Ⓗ "Russians celebrated the return of the treasures."

Name: _____   Date: _____

# A Royal Return to Russia *(cont.)*

**Directions:** Fill in the bubble of each correct answer choice.

4. The author includes the egg photograph and caption to show that . . .

   Ⓐ Easter eggs are important to Russians.

   Ⓑ the egg is both exquisite and expensive.

   Ⓒ these eggs belong in a museum.

   Ⓓ people deserve to see the eggs.

5. What can you infer from the text about Fabergé and his jewelers?

   Ⓐ They liked making birthday gifts.

   Ⓑ They were skilled artisans.

   Ⓒ They were well paid.

   Ⓓ They made other kinds of eggs.

6. Which sentence from the article best explains why the eggs are so important to Russians?

   Ⓐ "Fabergé created the first egg in 1885 for Czar Alexander III."

   Ⓑ "Together, the pieces are worth an estimated $100 million."

   Ⓒ "Fabergé eggs have long been the symbolic crown jewel of Russia's royal past."

   Ⓓ "The bounty included nine jeweled Faberge Easter eggs."

Name: _____ Date: _____

# A Royal Return to Russia *(cont.)*

**Directions:** Answer the questions.

7. Think about the kind of person Victor Vekselberg is. Based on the text, complete the graphic organizer with four adjectives about him.

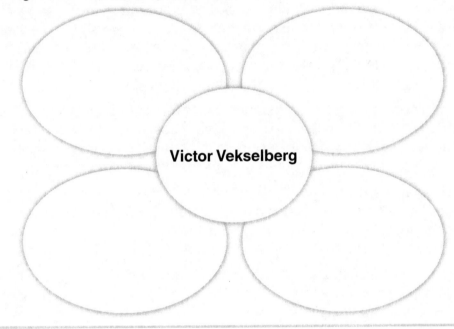

**Victor Vekselberg**

8. Choose one adjective from the web above. Use a quotation from the text to support why this adjective is a good description of Victor Vekselberg.

_____

_____

_____

_____

_____

Name: _____     Date: _____

# These Robots Are Wild

**Directions:** Read this text and respond to the questions on pages 40–42.

1   Most people think that cockroaches are nasty. But Roy Ritzmann has found a lot to love about them. "They're fast. They're agile," Ritzmann says. "And they're easy to take care of."

2   For Ritzmann, caring for cockroaches and other insects is more than just a quirky hobby. It is part of his job at Case Western Reserve University in Cleveland, Ohio. Ritzmann is a biologist. He helps other scientists at the school use bugs as models for robots. The scientists hope that new, insect-like robots will be able to operate where other robots can't.

3   "Many engineers now realize that much can be learned from biology," Roger Quinn told TIME For Kids. He is the director of Case Western Reserve's Biorobotics Laboratory. A group of robotics designers thinks that the behaviors and physical structures that help animals thrive could make machines more useful.

4   Arthropods are especially good robot models. Rugged arthropods include insects, crustaceans such as lobsters and crabs, and arachnids such as scorpions and spiders. Robotics scientists say arthropods have all the right moves. They are able to travel quickly over rocky or uneven ground.

5   Arthropods also have many sensors on the exteriors of their bodies. These sensors include antennas and fine, highly sensitive hairs. They help the creatures respond quickly to environmental changes.

# These Robots Are Wild (cont.)

## Acting Like a Bunch of Animals

6  Using animal-like sensors, the new robots will be able to react naturally in unpredictable environments. For example, they may find a path through a collapsed building to find the survivors of an earthquake. They have the ability to climb, crawl, or swim into dangerous situations or places.

7  Joseph Ayers is a biologist. He works at Northeastern University in Boston, Massachusetts. He has developed a robot based on the lobster. The U.S. military may one day use the RoboLobster to search for underwater mines. Mines are explosive devices. The way a lobster hunts for food is exactly the way you would want a robot to hunt for weapons. The lobster's sense of smell is strong. It locates its prey by following its scent along the ocean floor. Scientists are developing electronic sensors that work like a lobster's nose. Some can sniff out explosives underwater. Put such sensors on a robot, and you have a machine that is highly skilled at hunting down its prey—in this case, mines.

8  NASA scientists are thinking of making robots modeled after scorpions and cockroaches, too. They would be used to explore Mars. The new robots will travel over big boulders, down steep cliffs, and into tight spots. By acting like bugs, these robots may help humans unlock the mysteries of the universe.

*Roger Quinn (left) and Roy Ritzmann look at an early version of a roach-like robot.*

Name: _____ Date: _____

# These Robots Are Wild (cont.)

**Directions:** Fill in the bubble of each correct answer choice.

1. Which statements tell you why Roy Ritzmann thinks cockroaches are great? Choose all that apply.

   Ⓐ "They're fast. They're agile."

   Ⓑ "Rugged arthropods include insects."

   Ⓒ "And they're easy to take care of."

   Ⓓ "Most people think that cockroaches are nasty."

2. Which are examples of arthropods?

   Ⓐ insects and amphibians

   Ⓑ insects, snakes, and spiders

   Ⓒ insects, crustaceans, and mollusks

   Ⓓ insects, crustaceans, and arachnids

3. Which sentence supports the description of the arthropods being rugged?

   Ⓔ "Arthropods also have many sensors on the exterior of their bodies."

   Ⓕ "They are able to travel quickly over rocky or uneven ground."

   Ⓖ "Arthropods are especially good robot models."

   Ⓗ "Robotics scientists say arthropods have all the right moves."

Name: _____    Date: _____

# These Robots Are Wild (cont.)

**Directions:** Fill in the bubble of each correct answer choice.

**4.** What is the meaning of the word *prey* in paragraph 7?

   Ⓐ kill

   Ⓑ target

   Ⓒ hope

   Ⓓ want

**5.** What does the subhead on page 39 mean?

   Ⓐ The robots imitate animal behaviors.

   Ⓑ The biologists like using animals like lobsters to do dangerous missions.

   Ⓒ The robots can explore dangerous places.

   Ⓓ Scientists study animals that have useful skills.

**6.** Read this sentence from paragraph 7: "The way a lobster hunts for food is exactly the way you would want a robot to hunt for weapons." This quotation shows that . . .

   Ⓐ lobsters have a strong sense of smell.

   Ⓑ lobsters have the ability to grasp prey with their claws.

   Ⓒ scientists think that lobsters have skills worth imitating.

   Ⓓ scientists think that lobsters are efficient hunters.

Name: _____ Date: _____

# These Robots Are Wild *(cont.)*

**Directions:** Answer the questions.

**7.** Consider the four skills that arthropod robots may possess. They are listed in the first column. In the second column, write an example of an unpredictable environment where each skill would be helpful.

| Arthropod Skill | Environment Where It Would Be Useful |
|---|---|
| climbing | |
| crawling | |
| swimming | |
| smelling | |

**8.** Which sentence in the last paragraph summarizes the article? Explain your answer.

_____

_____

_____

_____

_____

_____

Name: _____     Date: _____

# Genghis Khan and the Mongol Empire

**Directions:** Read this text and respond to the questions on pages 45–47.

1   The largest empire the world has ever known was started by a man who began his life in a tent. His name as a boy was Temujin. He is famous today as Genghis Khan.

2   As a boy, Temujin was captured and made a slave by a rival tribe. He escaped slavery and lived as an outlaw. He was not especially strong, and he never learned to read. Yet he and his children led the Mongol army to conquere much of the known world. At its height, their empire stretched from China all the way west to the edge of Europe. To the south it stretched into most of the Middle East and parts of India.

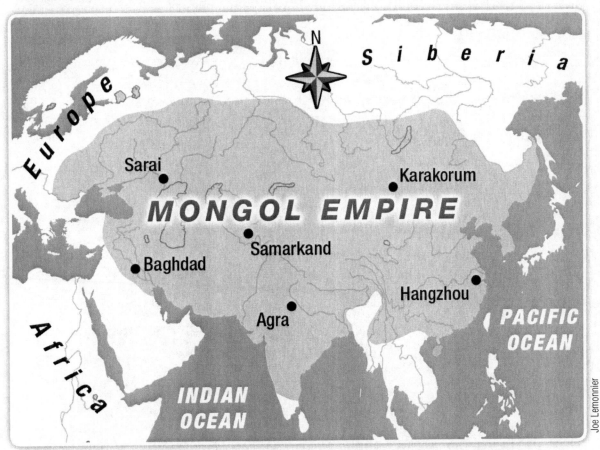

3   The Mongol army struck fear into its opponents by using tactics no one had ever seen before. They traveled quickly on horseback and relied on speed to defeat their enemies. They were experts of siege warfare, surrounding towns and breaking down their defenses. They were also quick to use new materials and methods. For example, they took gunpowder from China, changed it, and invented the cannon.

# Genghis Khan and the Mongol Empire *(cont.)*

4   Although the Mongols were ruthless in battle, as rulers they were fairly open minded. In their empire, there was freedom of religion. Government jobs were filled based on ability, not noble birth. The Mongols encouraged new ideas, new systems of writing, and scientific investigation. Under their rule, trade grew and skilled artists made beautiful objects. Art, culture, and learning traveled from one end of the empire to the other.

5   The most well-known story of the Mongol Empire was written by a businessman from Venice, Italy. His name was Marco Polo. Polo went to China in 1275 and lived for 17 years in the court of Kublai Khan, Genghis Khan's grandson. When Polo returned home, his reports of what he had seen helped spark European interest in the Far East.

6   The Mongol Empire did not last past Genghis Khan's grandsons. One major reason for its fall was the Black Plague that swept out of Asia and hit Europe in 1347, killing tens of thousands of people. Yet Khan's influence continued to be felt long after, both in the parts of the empire that survived and in the great trading of ideas and cultures that it had created.

North Wind Picture Archives/Alamy

*Genghis Khan riding into battle*

# Genghis Khan and the Mongol Empire (cont.)

**Directions:** Fill in the bubble of each correct answer choice.

1. Which sentence tells you that Genghis Khan had courage and stamina as a boy?

   Ⓐ "He is famous today as Genghis Khan."

   Ⓑ "His name as a boy was Temujin."

   Ⓒ "As a boy, Temujin was captured by a rival tribe."

   Ⓓ "He escaped slavery and lived as an outlaw."

2. What is the meaning of the word *conquer* in paragraph 2?

   Ⓐ judge

   Ⓑ fight

   Ⓒ inspire

   Ⓓ dominate

3. Which detail shows that the Mongols were creative?

   Ⓐ They used what they learned about gunpowder to invent the cannon.

   Ⓑ They were ruthless during battles, defeating their enemies.

   Ⓒ They let people choose their own religion.

   Ⓓ They had people earn their jobs based on their abilities.

Name: _____   Date: _____

# Genghis Khan and the Mongol Empire *(cont.)*

**Directions:** Fill in the bubble of each correct answer choice.

4. Read this sentence from paragraph 4: "Although the Mongols were ruthless in battle, as rulers they were fairly open minded." Why does the author include this information?

   Ⓐ It shows that the Mongols enjoyed being conquerors.

   Ⓑ It shows that Genghis Khan was a wise ruler.

   Ⓒ It shows that the Mongols had a tolerant side.

   Ⓓ It shows what Genghis Khan learned from being a slave.

5. Which sentence from the article serves a similar purpose?

   Ⓔ "At its height, their empire stretched from China all the way west to the edge of Europe."

   Ⓕ "The Mongols encouraged new ideas, new systems of writing, and scientific investigation."

   Ⓖ "They were also quick to use new materials and methods."

   Ⓗ "The Mongol army struck fear into its opponents by using tactics no one had ever seen before."

6. The author includes the map to show . . .

   Ⓐ where the Mongols fought for control.

   Ⓑ the extent of the Mongols' control.

   Ⓒ where Genghis Khan lived as an outlaw.

   Ⓓ the extent of the Black Plague.

Name: _____  Date: _____

# Genghis Khan and the Mongol Empire *(cont.)*

**Directions:** Answer the questions.

7.  The reign of the Mongols brought positive and negative changes to Asia and Europe. Using information from the text, complete the chart.

| Positive Influences | Negative Influences |
|---|---|
| 1. | 1. |
| 2. | 2. |
| 3. | 3. |

8.  Reread the last paragraph. Explain why the Khans continued to be influential after their empire ended.

_____

_____

_____

_____

Name: _____     Date: _____

# Greening Africa

**Directions:** Read this text and respond to the questions on pages 49–51.

1   Across northern Africa, the desert is steadily growing. Dry, parched lands are increasing. But a bold project known as the Great Green Wall aims to stop the spread of the desert. The ambitious program includes plans to help protect and maintain resources and fight poverty.

2   Farmers are learning to care for their land and use water wisely. They are also planting millions of trees and crops. The Great Green Wall will eventually cover an area more than 4,000 miles (6,437 km) long—from Senegal in the west to Djibouti in the east.

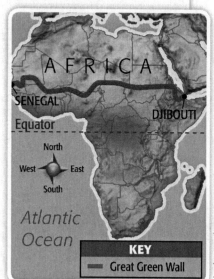

3   The Great Green Wall was first approved by the African Union, a group of 53 nations, in 2007. The program receives support from the United Nations, the World Bank, and other groups.

4   According to the United Nations Food and Agriculture Organization (FAO), about two-thirds of Africa is desert or dry land. Climate change has led to long periods of drought. Some areas that once had crops are no longer fertile. They cannot produce crops because the land was not properly taken care of.

5   The Great Green Wall's trees provide a barrier against desert winds and help hold moisture in the air and soil, allowing crops to grow. In time, the richer soil will provide more land for animals to graze on. More resources will bring more jobs.

6   "The goal is to create sustainable land management," Nora Berrahmouni, a forestry officer with the FAO, told TIME For Kids.

7   Trees and crops have been planted in Senegal and Niger. An added benefit of the Great Green Wall is that countries in the region are sharing information about which programs work and which don't. Now, along with trees, ideas are taking root.

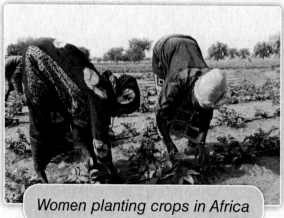

*Women planting crops in Africa*

Name: _____  Date: _____

# Greening Africa (cont.)

**Directions:** Fill in the bubble of each correct answer choice.

1.  Which sentence from the article explains the primary reason why the Great Green Wall is important?

    Ⓐ "Trees and crops have been planted in Senegal and Niger."

    Ⓑ "Across northern Africa, the desert is steadily growing."

    Ⓒ "In time, the richer soil will provide more land for animals to graze on."

    Ⓓ "Now, along with trees, ideas are taking root."

2.  Which fact from the article suggests that African farmers work hard?

    Ⓐ Farmers raise crops near the desert.

    Ⓑ Farmers need more water for their crops.

    Ⓒ Farmers are learning about the Great Green Wall.

    Ⓓ Farmers are planting millions of crops and trees.

3.  Why do you think the project is called the Great Green Wall?

    Ⓐ The project is made of growing things.

    Ⓑ The project is 4,000 miles (6,437 km) long.

    Ⓒ The project will help stop the desert.

    Ⓓ The project is in Djibouti and Senegal.

Name: _____    Date: _____

# Greening Africa (cont.)

**Directions:** Fill in the bubble of each correct answer choice.

4. Why is the map included in the article?

Ⓐ to show the nations in Africa

Ⓑ to describe the desert in Africa

Ⓒ to show where Sengal and Dijbouti are

Ⓓ to show the location of the Great Green Wall

5. What is the meaning of the word *ambitious* in paragraph 1?

Ⓐ well-organized

Ⓑ well-funded

Ⓒ large-scale

Ⓓ difficult

6. Which sentence from the text helps the reader to understand the meaning of *ambitious*?

Ⓔ "Climate change has led to long periods of drought."

Ⓕ "The Great Green Wall's trees provide a barrier against desert winds."

Ⓖ "The Great Green Wall will eventually cover an area more than 4,000 miles (6,437 km) long."

Ⓗ "Dry, parched lands are increasing."

Name: _____  Date: _____

# Greening Africa *(cont.)*

**Directions:** Answer the questions.

7.  What can you conclude about the success of the Great Green Wall project? Explain why you think it has or hasn't achieved its goals.

    _____

    _____

    _____

    _____

8.  Reread the last line of the article. Identify four good ideas or practices that are taking root because of this project. Write each one on a root of the tree.

Name: _____   Date: _____

# The Newsies Strike

**Directions:** Read this story and respond to the questions on pages 54–56.

1   "It's a scab! Get him!" The small boy standing on the street corner froze in fear. He was about 7 years old, and he was selling copies of *The Evening World* newspaper. He clutched his bundle of papers and looked for an escape route, but there was none.

2   Out of nowhere, dozens of boys came rushing toward the corner. The youngest was no more than 5; the oldest about 13. Like the paper seller, they were dressed in tattered jackets and wore breeches—short trousers that ended above their long socks. All wore caps of various shapes and colors. Their shoes thundered on the sidewalk. Men in business suits with starched collars and women in long dresses hurried to get out of the way.

3   The mob grabbed the poor paper seller. A large boy shook him by the lapels of his wool jacket while another knocked the bundle of papers out of his hands.

4   "Don't you know dere's a strike on?" the big boy asked angrily. "You know what we do ta scabs?"

5   "You lousy little scab!" yelled one of the strikers. "Teach him a lesson, Mike!"

6   "I didn't mean nuthin!" the paper seller cried, looking fearful for his life. "I got to make a livin', don't I?"

*Newsies selling their papers*

7   "Yeah, how you gonna make a livin' wid what they want to pay us?" asked another of the children. He snatched one of the papers from the ground and waved it about. "It was hard enough to make any dough when the papers cost a half-cent each. Now they raised the price. And you know if we don't sell 'em all, we're stuck with the leftovers."

# The Newsies Strike *(cont.)*

8　There was the murmur of angry agreement in the mob. Before the price hike, a newsboy could make about 25 cents a day, just barely enough to survive in New York City in 1899. Now that all the newspaper companies had raised the price of papers, it would be impossible to make even that much because fewer people would buy the expensive papers.

9　The little paper seller began to cry. Huge tears rolled down his dirty cheeks.

10　Mike's face softened. He let go of the strikebreaker's lapels. "What's your name?" he asked.

11　"Jack," the small boy whispered. "But everyone calls me Jackie."

12　"Look, Jackie," Mike said, "We ain't gonna hurt you, but you gotta promise to stick by the union from now on. All of us newsies gotta stick together, and that's how we'll win. Do ya see? Is it a promise?"

13　"Sure," Jackie said, his tears slowing. "I promise."

14　"Good," Mike replied, clapping him on the back. "Then come on with us and help spread the word."

15　Then they ran off, their feet thundering on the pavement.

*A young newsboy selling papers*

Library of Congress

Name: _____    Date: _____

# The Newsies Strike (cont.)

**Directions:** Fill in the bubble of each correct answer choice.

1. What can you infer from this sentence from paragraph 2: "Men in business suits with starched collars and women in long dresses hurried to get out of the way."?

   Ⓐ The adults are very careful about how they walk.

   Ⓑ The adults don't want to be involved with the newsies.

   Ⓒ The adults don't want to buy newspapers.

   Ⓓ The adults think the newsies should be in school.

2. What is the meaning of the word *scab* in paragraph 1?

   Ⓐ child worker

   Ⓑ crusty skin

   Ⓒ strikebreaker

   Ⓓ newspaper seller

3. The photographs best help the reader to visualize . . .

   Ⓐ the clothing and ages of the newsies.

   Ⓑ where the newsies sold papers.

   Ⓒ how the newsies felt about the strike.

   Ⓓ why the newsies sold papers.

Name: _____  Date: _____

# The Newsies Strike *(cont.)*

**Directions:** Fill in the bubble of each correct answer choice.

4.  What is the purpose of this sentence from paragraph 6: "I got to make a livin', don't I?"

    (A) The newspaper seller is angry about the price.

    (B) The newspaper seller relies on selling papers to survive.

    (C) The newspaper seller doesn't care about the strike.

    (D) The newspaper seller is afraid of the mob.

5.  Which sentence from the story serves a similar purpose?

    (E) "The little paper seller began to cry."

    (F) "He snatched one of the papers from the ground and waved it about."

    (G) "There was the murmur of angry agreement in the mob."

    (H) "It was hard enough to make any dough when the papers cost a half-cent each."

6.  Why does the author choose to use dialect in the story, such as in this sentence from paragraph 12: "We ain't gonna hurt you . . . ."

    (A) to show the difference between Jackie and Mike

    (B) to show that the boys like to have jobs

    (C) to show that the boys like to work as newsies

    (D) to show that the boys are not well educated

Name: _____     Date: _____

# The Newsies Strike *(cont.)*

**Directions:** Answer the questions.

7. There are two sides to every story. Complete the chart showing the opposing views of Jackie and Mike. Give two reasons for each boy.

| Jackie's Justifications for Selling Papers | Mike's Justifications for Supporting the Strike |
| --- | --- |
| | |

8. Who has the better reason for his actions, Jackie or Mike? Justify your response.

_____

_____

_____

_____

_____

Name: _____ Date: _____

# It Takes One to Know One

**Directions:** Read this story and respond to the questions on pages 59–61.

1. I looked through the one-way glass at the suspect. You couldn't tell by looking at him that he was a robot, but then he was one of the newest models, a J-class humanoid.

2. As I looked through the humanoid's e-file that Sergeant Culligan handed to me, I saw that the suspect went by the name of Carl 562 and had been leased to the Grovica Corporation as a computer technician. Makes sense, a robot to repair computers, right?

3. Except when the robot was accused of a crime. According to the e-file, this J-class robot had managed to transfer a very large amount of money out of the corporation's accounts.

4. "Has he said anything?" I asked.

5. "Nothing. Didn't even ask for a lawyer," Culligan replied. "Do robots get lawyers?"

6. "Anything above a D-class does," I said. "Let me see what I can do."

*Carl 562's interrogation*

Lynne Yoshi

# It Takes One to Know One (cont.)

7　I walked into the interrogation room and pulled up a chair. Now that I was sitting just a few feet away, I could see that he was very realistic. His black hair needed a trim, and there was sweat on his upper lip. I almost offered him a glass of water, but of course there was no point in that.

8　"So Carl," I said, "What would a robot, even a J-class robot, do with all that money?"

9　"I didn't transfer any money," he said, in a smooth baritone. "I'm not programmed for it."

10　"Oh, don't be modest," I said. "We both know you're capable of it."

11　"Just because I could do it doesn't mean I did," he responded. "Like you said, what would I do with money?"

12　"There was a case a few weeks ago of another J-class who stole money so she could buy her own lease." I watched to see his response. "Maybe you want your freedom."

13　"To do what?" Carl 562 replied calmly. "I like repairing computers."

14　"You mean, you're supposed to like it," I told him. "Maybe there's a bug in your program. Why don't you let us take out your memory chip . . . ."

15　"No!" Carl 562's face turned red. "I won't let you!"

16　"You don't have a choice," I said, reaching into my jacket for my tool kit. "Police officers are allowed to examine any robot's memory chip at any time."

17　Carl looked at the tool kit in fear. "Okay!" he cried. "I did it! I wanted to buy my own lease because I hate repairing stupid computers!" He started to cry very real-looking tears.

18　"Hey, don't go haywire," I said. "We'll see if we can't get you assigned to something else. Now, where's the money?"

19　Less than an hour later, the money was back where it belonged, and Carl 562 had been reprogrammed as a gardener. Maybe the fresh air would do him good.

20　"How did you know he would freak out over having his memory removed?" Culligan asked.

21　"Don't forget, Culligan," I replied, "that I am a J-class robot myself."

# It Takes One to Know One *(cont.)*

**Directions:** Fill in the bubble of each correct answer choice.

1. What is the meaning of *interrogation* as it is used in paragraph 7?

   Ⓐ conference

   Ⓑ examination

   Ⓒ questioning

   Ⓓ briefing

2. Read this sentence from paragraph 7: "His black hair needed a trim, and there was sweat on his upper lip." What is this sentence's purpose?

   Ⓐ to show how much Carl thinks like a human

   Ⓑ to show how much Carl responds like a human

   Ⓒ to show how much Carl moves like a human

   Ⓓ to show how much Carl talks like a human

3. Which sentence from the story serves a similar purpose?

   Ⓔ "Carl 562's face turned red."

   Ⓕ "Maybe the fresh air would do him good."

   Ⓖ "I like repairing computers."

   Ⓗ "I'm not programmed for it."

Name: _____ Date: _____

# It Takes One to Know One *(cont.)*

**Directions:** Fill in the bubble of each correct answer choice.

4. What can the reader conclude about Carl from this statement: "'I didn't transfer any money,' he said in a smooth baritone."

   Ⓐ Carl is programmed to be a computer technician.

   Ⓑ Carl is programmed to like the job he had.

   Ⓒ Carl is programmed to be truthful.

   Ⓓ Carl is programmed to speak with expression.

5. Which statement from the story is the turning point?

   Ⓐ "Why don't you let us take out your memory chip . . . ."

   Ⓑ "We both know you're capable of it."

   Ⓒ "Maybe there's a bug in your program."

   Ⓓ "Maybe you want your freedom."

6. How does the title relate to the story's resolution?

   Ⓐ The title shows why Carl 562 dislikes repairing computers.

   Ⓑ The title explains how the narrator can think like Carl 562.

   Ⓒ The title tells why humanoids look realistic.

   Ⓓ The title confirms why Carl 562 transfers the money.

Name: _____ Date: _____

# It Takes One to Know One (cont.)

**Directions:** Answer the questions.

7. Create an outline of the story by filling in each of the blanks.

**Setting** _____ **Time** _____

**Characters** _____

_____

**Problem** _____

**Events** _____

_____

_____

**Resolution** _____

_____

8. Authors sometimes end stories with unexpected twists. What is the twist at the end of this story? Support your response with a quotation from the text.

_____

_____

_____

_____

# The Man Who Never Lied

### Adapted from an African folktale

**Directions:** Read this story and respond to the questions on pages 64–66.

1  Once upon a time there lived a wise man by the name of Akili who was known throughout the land for his special virtue: he never told a lie. This piqued the king's interest, and he ordered Akili to appear at the palace. The king stared gravely at the wise man and said, "I have heard you never lie. Is that true?"

2  Akili answered, "Yes, that is true."

3  "And you will never lie for the rest of your life?" said the king, smirking skeptically.

4  "I can promise you that," replied Akili, without a hint of vanity.

5  "Good!" said the king. "I will hold you to your word."

6  The next week, Akili was summoned to the palace as the king readied to go hunting. The king had his left foot in his horse's stirrup, as if about to mount it. He commanded Akili, "Go to the summer palace and tell the queen I am going hunting today, but I will be there for a big feast at noon tomorrow." Akili bowed to the king and then traveled to the summer palace.

Francesca D'Ottavi

7  The king turned to his large retinue and said with a grim smile, "I am not going hunting, so Akili will lie to the queen. Tomorrow, he will be proven a liar, and I will have an enormous laugh at his expense."

# The Man Who Never Lied (cont.)

8 Within the labyrinth of the summer palace, Akili encountered the queen and told her, "I don't know if the king put his right foot in the stirrup and rode off hunting after I left, or if he put his left foot on the ground and stayed."

9 The queen said impatiently, "Well, is he coming for lunch tomorrow?"

10 "Maybe you should prepare a big feast for tomorrow; on the other hand, maybe you shouldn't. Maybe the king will come by noon, or maybe he won't. I can't say for certain."

11 The next day, the king arrived at the summer palace two hours late and told the queen with a smile, "Akili, the man who never lies, lied to you yesterday. I did not go hunting."

12 The queen responded, "Akili never said you did." When she told him what Akili did say, the king realized that a wise man never lies but states only what he can verify with his own eyes.

Francesca D'Ottavi

Name: _____ Date: _____

# The Man Who Never Lied (cont.)

**Directions:** Fill in the bubble of each correct answer choice.

1. Which sentence states the main idea of the first paragraph?

   Ⓐ Akili is the name of a well-known wise man.

   Ⓑ A king wants to meet a man named Akili.

   Ⓒ Akili appears at the palace to meet the king.

   Ⓓ A king is intrigued by a man who never tells lies.

2. What does the word *piqued* mean as it is used in paragraph 1?

   Ⓐ aroused

   Ⓑ stifled

   Ⓒ produced

   Ⓓ curbed

3. How is the dialogue important to understanding the story? Choose all that apply.

   Ⓐ It helps the reader to understand the king's attitude.

   Ⓑ It helps the reader to learn why Akili never lies.

   Ⓒ It helps the reader to understand how Akili avoids lying.

   Ⓓ It helps the reader to understand how the queen thinks.

Name: _____   Date: _____

# The Man Who Never Lied (cont.)

**Directions:** Fill in the bubble of each correct answer choice.

---

**4.** Choose two words that describe Akili.

   Ⓐ  noble

   Ⓑ  cooperative

   Ⓒ  humble

   Ⓓ  proud

**5.** Which sentence from the story supports the answer to number 4?

   Ⓔ  "Maybe you should prepare a big feast for tomorrow."

   Ⓕ  "'I can promise you that,' replied Akili, without a hint of vanity."

   Ⓖ  "Maybe the king will come by noon, or maybe he won't."

   Ⓗ  "Akili, the man who never lies, lied to you yesterday."

---

**6.** Which statement from the story best helps readers realize the king's true nature?

   Ⓐ  "The king stared gravely at the wise man and said, 'I have heard you never lie. Is that true?'"

   Ⓑ  "'And you will never lie for the rest of your life?' said the king, smirking skeptically."

   Ⓒ  "He commanded Akili, 'Go to the summer palace and tell the queen I am going hunting today . . .'"

   Ⓓ  "Tomorrow, he will be proven a liar, and I will have an enormous laugh at his expense."

Name: _____   Date: _____

# The Man Who Never Lied (cont.)

**Directions:** Answer the questions.

7. Why does the author include the line just below the title?

_____

_____

_____

_____

8. Determine the five key events in the story. Then, write them in the graphic organizer in the correct sequence.

| Event 1 | |
|---|---|
| Event 2 | |
| Event 3 | |
| Event 4 | |
| Event 5 | |

Name: _____   Date: _____

# The Embarrassing Episode of Little Miss Muffet

## by Guy Wetmore Carryl

**Directions:** Read this poem and respond to the questions on pages 68–70.

1   Little Miss Muffet discovered a tuffet,
(Which never occurred to the rest of us)
And as 'twas a June day, and just about noonday,
She wanted to eat—like the best of us.
Her diet was whey[1], and I hasten to say
It is wholesome and people grow fat on it.
The spot being lonely, the lady not only
Discovered the tuffet, but sat on it.

9   A rivulet gabbled beside her and babbled,
As rivulets always are thought to do,
And dragonflies sported around and cavorted,
As poets say dragonflies ought to do;
When glancing aside for a moment, she spied
A horrible sight that brought fear to her,
A hideous spider was sitting beside her,
And most unavoidably near to her!

17   Albeit unsightly, this creature politely
Said: "Madam, I earnestly vow to you,
I'm penitent that I did not bring my hat. I
Should otherwise certainly bow to you."
Though anxious to please, he was so ill at ease
That he lost all his sense of propriety,
And grew so inept that he clumsily stepped
In her plate—which is barred in society.

25   This curious error completed her terror;
She shuddered, and growing much paler, not
Only left tuffet but dealt him a buffet
Which doubled him up in a sailor knot.
It should be explained that at this he was pained:
He cried, "I have vexed you, no doubt of it!
Your fist's like a truncheon[2]!" "You're still in my luncheon,"
Was all that she answered. "Get out of it!"

33   And the moral is this: Be it madam or miss
To whom you have something to say,
You are only absurd when you get in the curd
But you're rude when you get in the whey!

[1]the watery part of milk left over after making cheese

[2]club

Name: _____ Date: _____

# The Embarrassing Episode of Little Miss Muffet *(cont.)*

**Directions:** Fill in the bubble of each correct answer choice.

1. What is the main idea of the first stanza?

   Ⓐ Whey is a good food for getting fat.

   Ⓑ Little Miss Muffet finds a place to have her lunch.

   Ⓒ A tuffet is a fine place for sitting.

   Ⓓ It is noon on a day in the month of June.

2. Why does the author organize the poem into stanzas?

   Ⓐ to show the characters' dialogue

   Ⓑ to use more alliteration

   Ⓒ to support the story line

   Ⓓ to support the rhyme and rhythm

3. Which lines from the poem let the reader know that the spider doesn't really mean to frighten Little Miss Muffet? Choose all that apply.

   Ⓐ "I'm penitent that I did not bring my hat."

   Ⓑ "Though anxious to please, he was so ill at ease"

   Ⓒ "That he lost all his sense of propriety"

   Ⓓ "It should be explained that at this he was pained"

Name: _____     Date: _____

# The Embarrassing Episode of Little Miss Muffet (cont.)

**Directions:** Fill in the bubble of each correct answer choice.

4. What is the meaning of the word *inept* as it is used in line 23?

   Ⓐ inefficient

   Ⓑ insignificant

   Ⓒ incompetent

   Ⓓ indifferent

5. Which of the sentences from the poem best helps the reader to understand the meaning of *inept*?

   Ⓔ "Which doubled him up in a sailor knot."

   Ⓕ "This curious error completed her terror."

   Ⓖ "You're still in my luncheon."

   Ⓗ "Only left tuffet but dealt him a buffet"

6. Why are there footnotes beneath the poem?

   Ⓐ to define unfamiliar words

   Ⓑ to provide more information

   Ⓒ to support reading the poem aloud

   Ⓓ to provide additional rhyming words

# The Embarrassing Episode of
# Little Miss Muffet (cont.)

**Directions:** Answer the questions.

7. Complete the senses chart by listing what Little Miss Muffet can see, hear, feel, taste, and smell. Include at least one item in each category.

| See | |
|-----|--|
| Hear | |
| Feel | |
| Taste | |
| Smell | |

8. How does the author use wordplay in the last line?

_____

_____

_____

_____

Name: _____     Date: _____

# Barbara Frietchie

## by John Greenleaf Whittier

**Directions:** Read this poem and respond to the questions on pages 73–75.

*Barbara Frietchie lived in Frederick, Maryland, during the Civil War. During September 1862, the Rebel forces occupied Frederick. Most residents simply endured the occupation, keeping quiet about their support of the Union. Although there is some debate as to exactly when and how Barbara Frietchie challenged the Rebels, historians agree that she showed her defiance.*

1   On that pleasant morn of the early fall
    When Lee marched over the mountain wall,—

2   Over the mountains winding down,
    Horse and foot, into Frederick town.

3   Forty flags with their silver stars,
    Forty flags with their crimson bars,

4   Flapped in the morning wind: the sun
    Of noon looked down, and saw not one.

5   Up rose old Barbara Frietchie then,
    Bowed with her fourscore years and ten;

6   Bravest of all in Frederick town,
    She took up the flag the men hauled down;

7   In her attic window the staff she set,
    To show that one heart was loyal yet.

8   Up the street came the rebel tread,
    Stonewall Jackson riding ahead.

9   Under his slouched hat left and right
    He glanced: the old flag met his sight.

10  "Halt!"—the dust-brown ranks stood fast.
    "Fire!"—out blazed the rifle-blast.

11  It shivered the window, pane and sash;
    It rent the banner with seam and gash.

12  Quick, as it fell, from the broken staff
    Dame Barbara snatched the silken scarf;

Barbara Frietchie

# Barbara Frietchie (cont.)

13  She leaned far out on the window-sill,
    And shook it forth with a royal will.

14  "Shoot, if you must, this old gray head,
    But spare your country's flag," she said.

15  A shade of sadness, a blush of shame,
    Over the face of the leader came;

16  The nobler nature within him stirred
    To life at that woman's deed and word:

17  "Who touches a hair on yon gray head
    Dies like a dog! March on!" he said.

18  All day long through Frederick street
    Sounded the tread of marching feet:

19  All day long that free flag tost
    Over the heads of the rebel host.

*Barbara Frietchie protected the flag.*

20  Ever its torn folds rose and fell
    On the loyal winds that loved it well;

21  And through the hill-gaps sunset light
    Shone over it with a warm good-night.

22  Barbara Frietchie's work is o'er,
    and the Rebel rides on his raids no more.

23  Peace and order and beauty draw
    'round thy symbol of light and law;

24  And ever the stars above look down
    On thy stars below in Frederick town!

# Barbara Frietchie (cont.)

**Directions:** Fill in the bubble of each correct answer choice.

1. Which detail from the poem tells you that Barbara Frietchie is old?

   Ⓐ "...bowed with her fourscore years and ten;"

   Ⓑ "...one heart was loyal yet."

   Ⓒ "...she took up the flag the men hauled down;"

   Ⓓ "Bravest of all in Frederick town,"

2. Reread the second and third stanzas. What can you conclude about the Union flags?

   Ⓐ that Rebel soldiers shot the flags

   Ⓑ that Union soldiers had removed all the flags

   Ⓒ that the townspeople had removed all the flags

   Ⓓ that the Union soldiers put the flags back up

3. Which lines show that Stonewall Jackson is in charge? Choose all that apply.

   Ⓐ "'Halt!'—the dust-brown ranks stood fast."

   Ⓑ "'Fire!'—out blazed the rifle-blast."

   Ⓒ "Up the street came the rebel tread,"

   Ⓓ "Under his slouched hat left and right / He glanced ...."

Name: _____ Date: _____

# Barbara Frietchie (cont.)

**Directions:** Fill in the bubble of each correct answer choice.

4. What is the meaning of the word *rent* as it is used in stanza 11?

   Ⓐ hired

   Ⓑ paid

   Ⓒ stopped

   Ⓓ ripped

5. Which of the sentences from the poem best helps the reader to understand the meaning of *rent*?

   Ⓔ "Quick as it fell from the broken staff Dame Barbara snatched the silken scarf."

   Ⓕ "All day long that free flag tost over the heads of the rebel host;"

   Ⓖ "Ever its torn folds rose and fell on the loyal winds that loved it well."

   Ⓗ "Peace and order and beauty draw 'round thy symbol of light and law;"

6. Which sentence from the poem is the climax?

   Ⓐ "Flapped in the morning wind: the sun of noon looked down and saw not one."

   Ⓑ "Under his slouched hat left and right he glanced, the old flag met his sight."

   Ⓒ "Now Barbara Frietchie's work is o'er and the Rebel rides on raids no more."

   Ⓓ "'Shoot, if you must, this old gray head, but spare your country's flag,' she said."

Name: _____ Date: _____

# Barbara Frietchie (cont.)

**Directions:** Answer the questions.

7. Complete the step-by-step chart by listing six key events from the poem.

**Step by Step**

| Event 1 | |
|---------|---|
| Event 2 | |
| Event 3 | |
| Event 4 | |
| Event 5 | |
| Event 6 | |

8. Do you think that the author supports the Union or the Rebel cause? Identify a line from the poem to justify your choice.

_____

_____

_____

Name: _____ Date: _____

# Anglezandria and the Golden Tri-Scarab

by Christi E. Parker

**Directions:** Read this script and respond to the questions on pages 79–81.

*In ancient Egypt, Pharaoh Rhombuses has called together a crowd.*

1 **Pentagonus:** Acutus, have you heard the news? Pharaoh Rhombuses is making an announcement today. Do you think it could be about the next heir to his throne?

**Acutus:** Maybe, but do you think farmers like us have a chance to become the next pharaoh?

**Pentagonus:** Our greatest love is math—something the pharaoh values, too. However, I don't know if a love for math could make either of us a ruler as great as a pharaoh.

**Acutus:** Here come two messengers. Let's listen to what they have to say.

5 **Pointus:** Attention all Anglezandrians! As you are aware, Anglezandria is a splendid city.

**Scalena:** But without a great leader, the city would be nothing. Listen and heed the pharaoh's challenge.

**Pharaoh:** Greetings to my people! As you know, I have no children of my own, so I want to ensure that I have control over who succeeds me when I'm too old to rule this great land. My successor must be someone who loves math and this great city as much as I do.

**Scalena:** The pharaoh's advisors have hidden a symbol of great value. It's the royal Golden Tri Scarab—a beetle in the shape of a triangle.

*A golden scarab*

# Anglezandria and the Golden Tri-Scarab *(cont.)*

**Pointus:** Riddles hidden around our great land contain clues to the Golden Tri-Scarab's hiding place. The first Anglezandrian to solve the riddles and find the Golden Tri-Scarab will be the next pharaoh.

10 **Pharaoh:** My scribe, Obtusum, will now read the first clue.

**Obtusum:** Places with height, width, and depth can be found both high and low. These places are where you will need to go. To begin your search, look for a prism with a rectangular or square face. Once you see the six matching sides, you'll know you're in the right place.

**Pharaoh:** You can find the answers to this riddle in our great city. May the best person win!

**Pentagonus:** Acutus, let's work together. You have superior knowledge of math, and I know this city and all of its structures like the back of my hand.

**Acutus:** The first part of the riddle mentioned height, width, and depth. The riddles must be located in three-dimensional shaped structures.

15 **Pentagonus:** The second part of the riddle says to find a prism made of squares or rectangles. It also states that the prism has six matching sides.

**Acutus:** A cube! Are there any structures in Anglezandria composed of cubes?

**Pentagonus:** The Temple of Luxcube! It has a large pillar in front that is built from stacked cubes.

**Narrator:** Pentagonus and Acutus race to the temple and search the pillar for clues.

**Acutus:** Pentagonus, I have found something that could be the next clue. It appears to be a piece of wrinkled paper. Read it!

20 **Pentagonus:** The greatest site in Anglezandria today has one square base on which to lie. The faces of four triangles are built mighty high, and the common vertex points toward the sky.

**Acutus:** We're talking about a three-dimensional shape with a square base and four triangular faces.

**Pentagonus:** Could you draw one for me in the sand?

**Acutus:** Sure. Start with the square base, like this. Can you see how the four triangular faces meet at the vertex?

**Pentagonus:** That looks like the Pyramids of Vertiza. If we travel by camel, we should arrive by evening.

# Anglezandria and the Golden Tri-Scarab (cont.)

25 **Narrator:** Scalena, who has been watching the contest, races to report to the pharaoh.

**Scalena:** Sir, I ran all the way from the Temple of Luxcube. The two leaders in the contest are local farmers named Acutus and Pentagonus. They have solved the first two riddles and are on their way to the Pyramids of Vertiza.

**Pharaoh:** How did they figure out these riddles so quickly?

**Scalena:** It's their teamwork that puts them ahead of the others. It seems that Pentagonus knows the city of Anglezandria very well and Acutus is very knowledgeable in math, especially geometry. The two help each other, which is why they can quickly solve the riddles.

**Pointus:** That must be true, Pharaoh. I have seen many of the other competitors around Anglezandria. They seem lost and confused. They hope to find the Golden Tri-Scarab on their own because they don't want to work with others.

30 **Pharaoh:** Pointus, keep an eye on our competitors, and let me know how they're doing. They only have three more clues to solve before they find the Golden Tri-Scarab.

Pyramids in Egypt

Name: _____ Date: _____

# Anglezandria and the Golden Tri-Scarab (cont.)

**Directions:** Fill in the bubble of each correct answer choice.

1. What is the meaning of the word *values* as used in line 3?

   Ⓐ cherishes

   Ⓑ evaluates

   Ⓒ estimates

   Ⓓ prices

2. Which sentence from the script best helps the reader to understand the meaning of *values*?

   Ⓔ "As you are aware, Anglezandria is a splendid city."

   Ⓕ "But without a great leader, the city would be nothing."

   Ⓖ " . . . I want to ensure that I have control over who succeeds me . . ."

   Ⓗ "My successor must be someone who loves math and this great city as much as I do."

3. What can you conclude about the pharoah?

   Ⓐ He uses shapes to build pyramids.

   Ⓑ He holds great power and likes math.

   Ⓒ He likes to read and write.

   Ⓓ He thinks the farmers will lose.

Name: _____ Date: _____

# Anglezandria and the
# Golden Tri-Scarab (cont.)

**Directions:** Fill in the bubble of each correct answer choice.

4. Which sentences show that Pentagonus and Acutus have a good strategy? Choose all that apply.

Ⓐ "It's their teamwork that puts them ahead of the others."

Ⓑ "I have seen many of the other competitors around Anglezandria."

Ⓒ "Pointus, keep an eye on our competitors, and let me know how they're doing."

Ⓓ "The two help each other, which is why they can quickly solve the riddles."

5. The purpose of the narrator's lines is to . . .

Ⓐ give background information.

Ⓑ describe the setting of the contest.

Ⓒ describe the actions of characters.

Ⓓ tell who is winning the contest.

6. Why does the author use names such as Pentagonus, Acutus, Pointus, Scalena, and Obtusum?

Ⓐ Those names were common in ancient Egypt.

Ⓑ Those names fit with the theme of solving math puzzles.

Ⓒ Those names sound silly and fun.

Ⓓ Those names give clues to finding the Golden Tri-Scarab.

Name: _____ Date: _____

# Anglezandria and the
# Golden Tri-Scarab (cont.)

**Directions:** Answer the questions.

7.  Use the text to complete this Venn diagram comparing and contrasting Acutus and Pentagonus with the other Anglezandrians.  Put two details in each section.

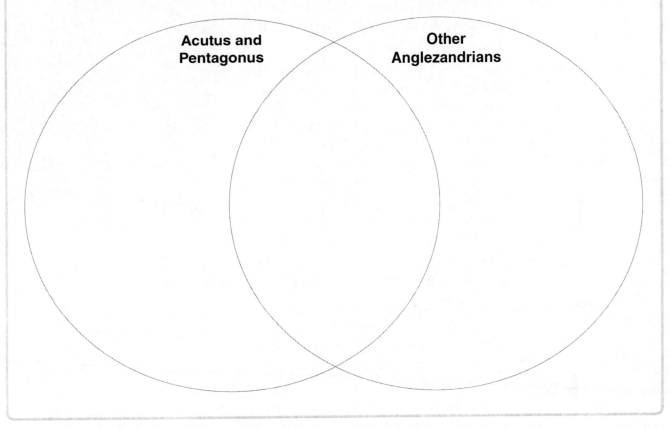

**Acutus and Pentagonus**

**Other Anglezandrians**

8.  Describe why Acutus and Pentagonus work well as a team. Use information from the script in your response.

_____

_____

_____

_____

_____

Name: _____   Date: _____

# Women's Suffrage

## by Dorothy Alexander Sugarman

> **Directions:** Read this script and respond to the questions on pages 85–87.

*The year is 1913, and women in the United States do not have the right to vote.*

*Carrie Catt*

1  **Narrator:** Many women have gathered at a meeting of the National American Women's Suffrage Association (NAWSA). Carrie Catt speaks to the group.

**Carrie Catt:** Quiet, everyone. Please, come to order! You know that we've had some trouble lately. Some of our members disagree with the leadership of this organization. They feel we are using the wrong tactics in our fight to get American women the right to vote, but we will never win if we spend our time arguing with one another. I would like everyone to understand what the NAWSA must do.

**Lucy Burns:** Carrie, we are certainly willing to listen to you. But, will you listen to us? We think that the NAWSA is wasting precious time.

**Carrie Catt:** Of course I will listen to your opinions, but we must come to an agreement today. We need to continue our work to change each state's constitution, state by state. It takes time and dedication. The fighting among us is wasting that time.

5  **Alice Paul:** Carrie, it is time to take a radical stand. As you know, from 1906 to 1909, I worked in England with the women's suffrage movement. We took part in protests. We took part in hunger strikes to bring attention and sympathy to our cause. These tactics are a better way of doing things. Working state by state is too slow. We must focus on the federal level and work for a United States constitutional amendment to give women the right to vote.

**Carrie Catt:** That's simply not possible! Don't you realize that it takes a two-thirds majority vote in both houses of Congress to pass a constitutional amendment? Then, the states have to ratify it. We'll never get the necessary votes for that.

**Lucy Burns:** We have an idea that will bring us national attention.

**Carrie Catt:** Protests and hunger strikes will just turn people against us.

# Women's Suffrage (cont.)

**Alice Paul:** We have decided that we must hold a huge suffrage parade in Washington on the day before Woodrow Wilson's inauguration. The parade will be massive, and the president will have to listen.

10 **Carrie Catt:** Stop! I cannot let this continue. The NAWSA will not sponsor such a parade. We must think about the consequences of our actions. We cannot afford to jeopardize what we have worked so hard to achieve. If you insist on continuing, you will be expelled from this organization.

**Alice Paul:** Carrie, we insist. If we must, we will start a new organization. We will organize this parade, and I will speak to Woodrow Wilson personally. He will not be able to ignore us!

**Narrator:** The NAWSA continued its work to change state constitutions. Alice and Lucy formed the Congressional Union. Later, they joined another group, becoming the National Woman's Party. On May 3, 1913, Woodrow Wilson arrived for his inauguration, which would take place the following day. Thousands of people lined Pennsylvania Avenue. Rows of women dressed in white marched and chanted. Since the president-elect's car could not move because the marchers were in the way, Woodrow Wilson got out of the car.

**Wilson:** I wonder what's going on. I certainly didn't expect a parade of women. It sounds like someone is giving a speech.

**Alice Paul:** Thank you for coming to the women's suffrage parade. The estimates are that between 5,000 and 8,000 women are marching today. It is high time for women to have the right to vote. We should have the right to make decisions and to vote for our leaders.

15 **Heckler:** What are you women up to? Women know nothing about politics, and they don't know how the government should run. A woman's work is in the home.

# Women's Suffrage (cont.)

**Wilson:**
*(to himself)*
These women couldn't have picked a worse time. I need the country to support me. This parade may ruin my inauguration! I must talk to the leader.

**Wilson:** Who organized this parade?

**Alice Paul:** I did, Mr. President.

**Wilson:** Do you realize the danger you all are in?

20 **Alice Paul:** Yes, sir, but we are not afraid. We have come voluntarily. Granting women the right to vote is essential. You must help us. We need you to act decisively on our behalf. I have something important to show you.

**Wilson:** What do you have to show me, and exactly what is it that you want me to do?

**Alice Paul:** I have a petition with 200,000 signatures from around the country. These people want a constitutional amendment that will give all women the right to vote.

**Wilson:** I believe it is up to each state to decide whether women should vote.

**Alice Paul:** But Mr. President, it should not be up to each state to decide. Every woman deserves the right to vote. It's why we need a constitutional amendment.

25 **Wilson:** I will try. But, there are a few things you must understand. There are many people who don't agree with what you want, and my job as president is just beginning. Passing an amendment to the Constitution is very, very difficult.

**Alice Paul:** Mr. President, I know it is difficult, but I will take that as a promise. I am counting on you to do the right thing.

**Heckler:** Mr. President, I cannot believe you are going to do this. Most men oppose the ideas of these women.

**Wilson:** Don't worry, sir. I'm quite sure that this issue will die over the next four years.

**Narrator:** But the issue did not die. On January 10, 1918, the Nineteenth Amendment passed in the House of Representatives. It passed in the Senate on June 4, 1919. On August 26, 1920, Tennessee, the last state that needed to ratify the amendment, voted for it. At last, women all over America could vote.

# Women's Suffrage (cont.)

**Directions:** Fill in the bubble of each correct answer choice.

1. Which statement best summarizes Carrie Catt's plan for gaining the right to vote?

   Ⓐ " . . . we will never win if we spend our time arguing with one another."

   Ⓑ "We cannot afford to jeopardize what we have worked so hard to achieve."

   Ⓒ "Protests and hunger strikes will just turn people against us."

   Ⓓ "We need to continue our work to change each state's constitution, state by state."

2. What does the word *tactics* means as it is used in line 2?

   Ⓐ tricks

   Ⓑ strategies

   Ⓒ systems

   Ⓓ plots

3. Which statement ignites the conflict that leads to a split in the NAWSA?

   Ⓐ "We need to continue our work to change each state's constitution, state by state."

   Ⓑ "We took part in hunger strikes to bring attention and sympathy to our cause."

   Ⓒ "We have decided that we must hold a huge suffrage parade in Washington . . . ."

   Ⓓ " . . . we will never win if we spend our time arguing with one another."

Name: _____   Date: _____

# Women's Suffrage (cont.)

**Directions:** Fill in the bubble of each correct answer choice.

4.  Which statement from Woodrow Wilson shows his position on a woman's right to vote?

    (A) " . . . there are a few things you must understand."

    (B) "I believe it is up to each state to decide whether women should vote."

    (C) "These women couldn't have picked a worse time."

    (D) "I certainly didn't expect a parade of women."

5.  Which statements made by Woodrow Wilson support the answer to number 4? Choose all that apply.

    (E) "This parade may ruin my inauguration!"

    (F) "I need the country to support me."

    (G) "I'm quite sure that this issue will die over the next four years."

    (H) "Passing an amendment to the Constitution is very, very difficult."

6.  How does this script compare to an informational text on the same topic?

    (A) The drama makes the reader feel as if he or she is part of the action.

    (B) The drama explores the internal motivation of the characters.

    (C) An informational text would include only facts.

    (D) An informational text would show the author's biased viewpoint.

Name: _____ Date: _____

# Women's Suffrage *(cont.)*

**Directions:** Answer the questions.

7. Use the text to complete this Venn diagram comparing and contrasting Carrie Catt and Alice Paul. Include two details in each section.

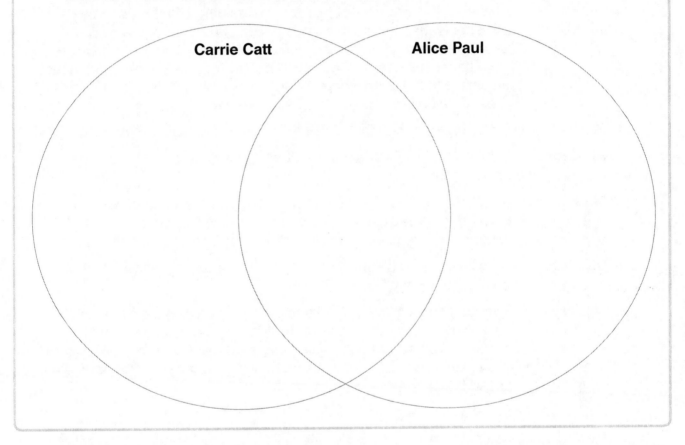

**Carrie Catt**          **Alice Paul**

8. Why is Alice Paul successful at being heard? Use at least three details from the text to support your opinion.

_____

_____

_____

_____

_____

Drama Practice Exercise

# Arthur and the Pendragon Sword
## by Debra J. Housel

**Directions:** Read this script and respond to the questions on pages 90–92.

*Merlin, a sorcerer, convinces King Pendragon that his newborn son is in danger. How will Merlin ensure the child's right to one day rule Britain?*

1 **Narrator:** More than 1,500 years ago Britain was led by Uther Pendragon, a wise king. It was a time of peace and prosperity, for he was such a powerful leader that none dared challenge him. Uther married the Lady Igraine, and in time, they welcomed a son. Merlin, a sorcerer and Uther's most trusted advisor, foresaw that the couple would meet an untimely end. Within hours of the baby's birth, Merlin convinced Uther to relinquish the newborn for safekeeping.

**Merlin:** Sir Ector, thank you for meeting me here under cover of darkness.

**Sir Ector:** I am His Majesty's loyal subject; I never hesitate when he requests an audience.

**Merlin:** King Uther has asked me to meet you in the presence of Sir Ulfius, his trusted seneschal. He has a consequential request to make of you, one that requires your utmost secrecy and utter devotion.

5 **Sir Ector:** His Majesty's wish is my command; I would do anything for him— even lay down my life.

**Merlin:** The King desires that you take his infant son and raise him as your own. You must love him, protect him, and teach him the code of chivalry, even as you do for your own son, Kai. Value the child's life above your own, for he is your sovereign, and the future of our nation lies with him.

**Sir Ector:** But why am I engaged in this subterfuge?

**Merlin:** You may ask no questions. The child's name is Arthur. You shall not see me again for many years, but when the time is right, all shall be revealed. Do you agree to undertake this task and solemnly swear on Kai's life that you and your wife shall keep this secret unto death?

**Sir Ector:** I solemnly swear to do this for my sovereign.

10 **Merlin:** Sir Ulfius, you bear witness to this most serious and sacred pact.

**Narrator:** Sir Ector took Arthur home and moved the family to Wales. Since no one knew them there, everyone accepted that they had two sons. Sir Ector's wife nursed the babe along with their child. Each night as she rocked Arthur to sleep, she quietly sang him a song about his birthright.

# Arthur and the Pendragon Sword *(cont.)*

**Merlin:** Within a year, King Uther and his wife lay dead from a traitor's poison, and for the next seventeen years, Britain endured violence and chaos as kings, dukes, and lords fought for control.

**Archbishop:** Merlin, we must discuss a grievous matter. Our homeland is in a state of anarchy as sectarian kings fight ceaselessly for control with none being powerful enough or wise enough to unite and guide the nation. The peasants are murdered by one marauding army and then another. Can you devise some means to restore our tortured realm?

**Merlin:** The nation shall soon have a king who shall be even wiser and greater and more worthy of praise than Uther Pendragon. Indeed, this king shall be of his own blood.

15 **Archbishop:** How can that be when Uther Pendragon left no heir? And how shall we recognize this man as the rightful king?

**Merlin:** Uther Pendragon did leave an heir who has been raised in secrecy, and he is now 18 years old. If you allow the use of magic, I shall set a task so impossible that the only man who can achieve it is this heir, the rightful high king and overlord of the realm.

**Archbishop:** I urge you to do whatever you believe right.

**Narrator:** That night, Merlin created a huge white marble slab in the cathedral's square. Upon the slab he placed an anvil, and into the anvil he thrust the blade of Uther's own Pendragon sword. The next day Merlin visited the Archbishop.

**Merlin:** This sword is the most magnificent in the land, for its blade is of purest blue steel and its hilt of gold inlaid with rubies, sapphires, and emeralds. With this sword Uther Pendragon vanquished his enemies and established his kingdom.

20 **Archbishop:** This is truly astonishing, Merlin! And look what you have engraved upon the marble: *Whosoever Pulleth Out This Sword from the Anvil Is the Rightwise King Born of Britain.*

**Merlin:** Only one in all the land can remove this sword. When he does so, the world shall know he is Uther Pendragon's son.

Name: _____   Date: _____

# Arthur and the Pendragon Sword (cont.)

**Directions:** Fill in the bubble of each correct answer choice.

1.  Which detail from the script proves that Uther Pendragon trusts Merlin?

    (A) "More than 1,500 years ago Britain was led by Uther Pendragon, a wise king."

    (B) " . . . Merlin convinced Uther to relinquish the newborn for safekeeping."

    (C) "It was a time of peace and prosperity, for he was such a powerful leader that none dared challenge him."

    (D) "Merlin, a sorcerer and Uther's most trusted advisor, foresaw that the couple would meet an untimely end."

2.  What can you conclude about Sir Ector's character from his actions?

    (A) He is too fearful to ask many questions.

    (B) He is living under a spell cast by Merlin.

    (C) He is devoted to Uther Pendragon.

    (D) He hopes to become rich and powerful.

3.  Which sentence from the drama best suggests that Merlin has the ability to see into the future?

    (A) "Within a year, King Uther and his wife lay dead from a traitor's poison . . . ."

    (B) "Sir Ector took Arthur home and moved the family to Wales."

    (C) "Uther married the Lady Igraine, and in time, they welcomed a son."

    (D) " . . . Merlin created a huge white marble slab in the cathedral's square."

Name: _____  Date: _____

# Arthur and the Pendragon Sword (cont.)

**Directions:** Fill in the bubble of the correct answer choice.

4. What is the meaning of the word *anarchy* as it is used in line 13?

Ⓐ revolution

Ⓑ disorder

Ⓒ protest

Ⓓ disapproval

5. Which sentence from the script best helps the reader to understand the meaning of *anarchy*?

Ⓔ " . . . Britain endured violence and chaos as kings, dukes, and lords fought for control."

Ⓕ "The nation shall soon have a king who shall be even wiser and greater and more worthy of praise than Uther Pendragon."

Ⓖ "The peasants are murdered by one marauding army and then another."

Ⓗ " . . . Merlin convinced Uther to relinquish the newborn for safekeeping."

6. The purpose of the narrator's lines is to . . .

Ⓐ describe the settings.

Ⓑ explore the characters' thoughts.

Ⓒ show the author's viewpoint.

Ⓓ summarize the action over time.

Name: _____ Date: _____

# Arthur and the Pendragon Sword *(cont.)*

**Directions:** Answer the questions.

7. Think about the kind of person Sir Ector is. Based on the script, complete the graphic organizer with four adjectives about him.

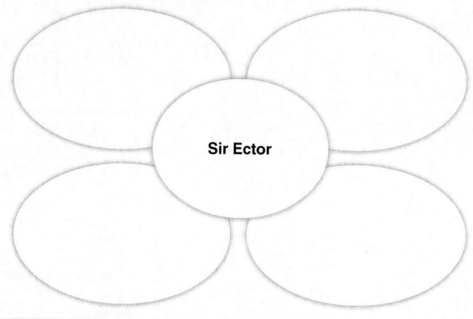

Sir Ector

8. Why does Merlin play such an important role in the script? Use information from the text to support your ideas.

_____

_____

_____

_____

_____

Name: _____     Date: _____

# The Bees and the Beetle
## an Aesop fable

**Directions:** Read this passage and respond to the questions on page 94.

1   Once some bees built a fine honeycomb filled with delicious honey in a hollow tree trunk. Two different types of bees live in a hive: the worker bees, which spend their lives gathering pollen and making honey, and the drones, which lie around doing absolutely nothing. The drones can't even be bothered with feeding themselves; instead, the workers feed them.

2   The drones boasted that they had made the finest honeycomb and most scrumptious honey ever seen or tasted. Their bragging angered the worker bees. They called in a wise old beetle to decide which bees had built the beautiful honeycomb and made the luscious honey.

3   "I cannot say for certain which of you built the honeycomb," said the beetle thoughtfully, "for you all look alike. Why don't you each move to a new location, establish a new hive, and create a new honeycomb. Once the honeycombs are complete, from the shape of the cells and the taste of the honey I can easily determine who built this fine honeycomb."

4   "That's not fair," protested the drone bees. "We don't want to have to build another honeycomb. We are talking about this honeycomb, not some new honeycomb."

5   "We'll get started immediately," said the worker bees. "We can probably finish it within twelve days."

6   The beetle said, "That won't be necessary. Since you are willing and eager to demonstrate your skills, it's obvious that this fine honeycomb and honey were created by you worker bees."

Name: _____ Date: _____

# The Bees and the Beetle (cont.)

**Directions:** Fill in the bubble of each correct answer choice.

1. Which elements of the story make it clear that it is a fable?

   Ⓐ The main characters are animals who have a problem.

   Ⓑ The setting is outside, and the story is very short.

   Ⓒ The animals act realistically.

   Ⓓ The animals talk like humans, and the story teaches a lesson.

2. The turning point in the story happens when . . .

   Ⓐ the bees argue about who made the honeycomb.

   Ⓑ the beetle tells the bees to create a new honeycomb.

   Ⓒ the beetle says that they all look alike.

   Ⓓ the worker bees feed the drones.

3. Which moral best fits this story?

   Ⓐ One good turn deserves another.

   Ⓑ Try to please all and you end up pleasing none.

   Ⓒ One's actions speak louder than one's words.

   Ⓓ Half a loaf is better than none.

Name: _____   Date: _____

# Abuzz at a Hotel

**Directions:** Read this text and respond to the questions on page 96.

1   One of New York City's fanciest hotels is home to more than 300,000 honeybees. Their hives are high above midtown Manhattan. They live on the 20th-floor roof of the Waldorf Astoria. The hotel's six beehives are abuzz with activity. According to the Waldorf's head chef, David Garcelon, the hives have produced hundreds of pounds of honey so far this year.

2   The honey is an ingredient in the Waldorf's pastries, ice cream, salad dressings, and soups. It is also used in many of its main-course dishes. "It's great for us to have our own source of honey," Garcelon told TIME For Kids. "We use it in all of our restaurants."

3   The beehives share the rooftop with a garden. Flowers, herbs, tomatoes, strawberries, apples, and other fruits and vegetables grow there. Andrew Coté is a professional beekeeper. He maintains the beehives at the Waldorf. He says having flowers nearby is good for honeybees. It gives them sources of nectar, which they need to make honey and to survive. The type of flower a bee collects nectar from is what gives the honey its distinctive flavor.

*Beekeeper Andrew Coté takes care of the beehives on top of the Waldorf Astoria hotel.*

4   When the weather turns colder, the Waldorf bees' busy season winds down. Bees are most active in the spring and summer. In the winter, the insects stay in their hives. They beat their wings to stay warm. They don't move around much.

## It's a Sweet City

5   The Waldorf's rooftop is actually just one of many in New York City that has beehives. "Beekeeping is a popular hobby throughout the city and in other cities around the world," Coté says.

6   A law once banned beekeeping in New York City. It was dropped in 2010. Since then, New Yorkers have set up hives and welcomed honeybees. People are pleased to produce and eat local honey. The bees also give city folks a taste of the country. As Coté says, "It's nice to be able to connect to nature when you are in the city."

Todd Plitt

Name: _____  Date: _____

# Abuzz at a Hotel (cont.)

**Directions:** Fill in the bubble of each correct answer choice.

4. The article is mainly about how . . .

   Ⓐ people in New York City keep bees as a hobby.

   Ⓑ bees adapt to the changing seasons.

   Ⓒ a hotel chef and beekeeper do their jobs.

   Ⓓ having a beehive at a hotel is beneficial.

5. Why does the author include the quotations in the article? Choose all that apply.

   Ⓐ They help the reader to understand what happens to bees in winter.

   Ⓑ They help the reader to understand the importance of the bees.

   Ⓒ They help the reader to understand the laws about beekeeping.

   Ⓓ They help the reader to understand how the honey is used.

6. The photo best supports which idea from the article?

   Ⓐ "The beehives share the rooftop with a garden."

   Ⓑ "The bees also give city folks a taste of the country."

   Ⓒ "Bees are most active in the spring and summer."

   Ⓓ "It's great for us to have our own source of honey."

Name: _____ Date: _____

# The Bees and the Beetle
## and Abuzz at a Hotel

**Directions:** Reread the texts on pages 93 and 95, and fill in the bubble of each correct answer choice.

7. How do the main ideas between the fable and the article differ?

   Ⓐ The main idea of the fable is a moral about work; the main idea of the article is the contribution of the bees at a hotel.

   Ⓑ The main idea of the fable is to teach a lesson; the main idea of the article is to convince people to keep bees.

   Ⓒ The main idea of the fable is a moral about greed; the main idea of the article is about using honey in food.

   Ⓓ The main idea of the fable is about how bees live in nature; the main idea of the article is about how bees live in a city.

8. Check all that apply. Both the fable and the article show that bees . . .

   Ⓐ are less active during winter.

   Ⓑ work hard to make honey.

   Ⓒ are valued for their honey.

   Ⓓ need nectar to make honey.

9. The authors wrote these pieces most likely to . . .

   Ⓐ teach a lesson and describe how bees make honey.

   Ⓑ teach about building honeycombs and describe how a chef uses honey.

   Ⓒ teach about a hobby and describe how beekeepers work.

   Ⓓ teach a moral and describe an unusual place for a beehive.

*#51439—TIME For Kids: Practicing for Today's Tests*

Name: _____     Date: _____

# Sympathy

## by Paul Laurence Dunbar

**Directions:** Read this poem and respond to the questions on page 99.

1    I know what the caged bird feels, alas!
     When the sun is bright on the upland slopes;
     When the wind stirs soft through the springing grass,
     And the river flows like a stream of glass;
     When the first bird sings and the first bud opens,
     And the faint perfume from its chalice steals—
     I know what the caged bird feels!

8    I know why the caged bird beats his wing
     Till its blood is red on the cruel bars;
     For he must fly back to his perch and cling
     When he fain would be on the bough a-swing;
     And a pain still throbs in the old, old scars
     And they pulse again with a keener sting—
     I know why he beats his wing!

15   I know why the caged bird sings, ah me,
     When his wing is bruised and his bosom sore—
     When he beats his bars and he would be free;
     It is not a carol of joy or glee,
     But a prayer that he sends from his heart's deep core,
     But a plea, that upward to heaven he flings—
     I know why the caged bird sings!

Name: _____     Date: _____

# Sympathy *(cont.)*

**Directions:** Fill in the bubble of each correct answer choice.

1. What does the word *bough* mean as it is used in the second stanza?

   Ⓐ nest

   Ⓑ branch

   Ⓒ perch

   Ⓓ landing

2. Read line 21: "I know why the caged bird sings!" Which part of the poem best summarizes the meaning of this statement?

   Ⓐ "When the wind stirs soft through the springing grass, / And the river flows like a stream of glass;"

   Ⓑ "When the first bird sings and the first bud opens, / And the faint perfume from its chalice steals—"

   Ⓒ "For he must fly back to his perch and cling / When he fain would be on the bough a-swing;"

   Ⓓ "It is not a carol of joy or glee, / But a prayer that he sends from his heart's deep core,"

3. What structure and pattern of poetry appear in this poem? Choose all that apply.

   Ⓐ free verse

   Ⓑ stanzas

   Ⓒ rhyming

   Ⓓ alliteration

Name: _____   Date: _____

# She Never Stopped Fighting:
# Shirley Chisholm

**Directions:** Read this text and respond to the questions on page 102.

1   What does it take to be the first? What does it take to fight for what you believe in, no matter what the odds? Whatever that quality is, Shirley Chisholm had it.

2   She was the first African American woman ever elected to the United States House of Representatives. From 1969 until 1983, she represented a section of Brooklyn, New York. During that time, she was a founding member of the Congressional Black Caucus. She worked tirelessly for the people in her district.

## Her Greatest Asset

3   Chisholm was born in New York City on November 30, 1924. Her parents had moved there from the Caribbean. After college, she worked as a nursery school teacher. Then she was the director of a day care center. In 1964, she won a seat in the New York State Assembly.

*Shirley Chisholm*

Wally McNamee/Corbis

4   From the moment she entered Congress in 1969, Chisholm was not content to go along with politics as usual. When she was assigned to a committee on agriculture, she objected. She stated that she needed to work on issues that affected her urban district. Such refusals were unheard of. Still, Chisholm was assigned to a different committee.

5   She was in office during a time of great political turmoil. She was never afraid to speak out. Chisholm opposed the war in Vietnam. She fought for women's rights and the rights of minorities. "My greatest political asset, which professional politicians fear, is my mouth," she said.

# She Never Stopped Fighting:
# Shirley Chisholm (cont.)

## Shirley for President

6  In 1972, Chisholm achieved another first. She was the first African American to run for the presidential nomination of a major party. She won 152 delegates at the Democratic Party's convention. Then she withdrew from the race.

7  "I ran for the presidency, despite hopeless odds, to demonstrate the sheer will and refusal to accept the status quo," she later wrote. She hoped that her campaign would open the door to other women and minorities to run in the future.

8  After her presidential bid, Shirley Chisholm continued to fight for the poor. In 1974, she helped pass a new minimum-wage law. It covered maids and other domestic workers.

## She Had Guts

9  Chisholm described her approach to life by saying, "You don't make progress by standing on the sidelines, whimpering and complaining."

10 Chisholm died in 2005. She was 80 years old. Civil-rights leader Jesse Jackson called her a "woman of great courage . . . who refused to accept the ordinary." Shirley Chisholm stated how she wanted to be remembered: "I'd like them to say that Shirley Chisholm had guts."

*Chisholm fought for the rights of others.*

Name: _____ Date: _____

# She Never Stopped Fighting: Shirley Chisholm *(cont.)*

**Directions:** Fill in the bubble of each correct answer choice.

4. What is the meaning of *asset* as used in paragraph 5?

   Ⓐ strength

   Ⓑ property

   Ⓒ achievement

   Ⓓ possession

5. What is the purpose of the subheadings?

   Ⓐ to summarize the article

   Ⓑ to highlight her accomplishments

   Ⓒ to show the sequence of the article

   Ⓓ to organize the article by topic

6. What can the reader conclude about Shirley Chisholm?

   Ⓐ She enjoyed being a nursery school teacher.

   Ⓑ She devoted her life to fighting for others.

   Ⓒ She thought that being in politics was hard.

   Ⓓ She knew what it was like to be poor.

# Sympathy and She Never Stopped Fighting: Shirley Chisholm

**Directions:** Reread the texts on pages 98 and 100–101, and fill in the bubble of each correct answer choice.

7.  What sentence from the article shows that Shirley Chisholm was like the bird in the poem? Choose all that apply.

    (A) "I ran for the presidency, despite hopeless odds."

    (B) " . . . Chisholm was not content to go along with politics as usual."

    (C) "She was never afraid to speak out."

    (D) "She fought for women's rights and the rights of minorities."

8.  Chisholm worked to open doors for others, which was an important aspect of her life. Which line from "Sympathy" shows an important aspect of the bird's life?

    (A) "And the river flows like a stream of glass"

    (B) "For he must fly back to his perch and cling"

    (C) "When the first bird sings and the first bud opens"

    (D) "It is not a carol of joy or glee"

9.  Both the poem and the article express the power and frustration of . . .

    (A) working for others.

    (B) opening windows.

    (C) being able to speak out.

    (D) fighting against the odds.

# References Cited

Conley, David T. 2014. "Common Core Development and Substance." *Social Policy Report* 28 (2): 1–15.

Kornhaber, Mindy L., Kelly Griffith, and Alison Tyler. 2014. "It's Not Education by Zip Code Anymore—But What is It? Conceptions of Equity under the Common Core." *Education Policy Analysis Archives* 22(4): 1–26. doi:10.14507/epaa.v22n4.2014.

National Governors Association Center for Best Practices, Council of Chief State School Officers. 2010. *Common Core State Standards*. National Governors Association Center for Best Practices, Council of Chief State School Officers: Washington D.C. http://www.corestandards.org/about-the-standards/frequently-asked-questions/.

Partnership for Assessment of Readiness for College and Careers. 2013. *The PARCC Assessment.* PARCC: Washington, D.C. http://www.parcconline.org/about-parcc.

Rothman, Robert. 2013. *Common Core State Standards 101*. http://all4ed.org/reports-factsheets/common-core-state-standards-101/.

Texas Education Agency. 2014. *State of Texas Assessment of Academic Readiness: A Parent's Guide to the Student Testing Program.* TEA: Texas.

The Smarter Balanced Assessment Consortium. 2014. *Smarter Balanced Assessment Consortium.* California Department of Education. http://www.smarterbalanced.org/about/member-states/.

Wiley, Terrence G. and Wayne E. Wright. 2004. "Against the Undertow: Language-Minority Education Policy and Politics in the 'Age of Accountability.'" *Educational Policy*, 18 (1): 142–168. doi:10.1177/0895904803260030.

# Question Types

The following chart correlates each question in this book to one of the three types of questions. For more information on the types of questions, see pages 7–9.

| Practice Exercise Title | Item | Key Ideas and Details | Craft and Structure | Integration of Knowledge and Ideas |
|---|---|---|---|---|
| **But What Did They Write About?** (pages 13–17) | 1 | x | | |
| | 2 | x | | |
| | 3 | | | x |
| | 4 | | x | |
| | 5 | | x | |
| | 6 | x | | |
| | 7 | x | | |
| | 8 | x | | |
| **Peggy Whitson's Long Road to Space** (pages 18–22) | 1 | x | | |
| | 2 | x | | |
| | 3 | x | | |
| | 4 | | x | |
| | 5 | | x | |
| | 6 | | | x |
| | 7 | | x | |
| | 8 | x | | |
| **Science and the Environment: Are They Enemies?** (pages 23–27) | 1 | | | x |
| | 2 | | x | |
| | 3 | | x | |
| | 4 | x | | |
| | 5 | x | | |
| | 6 | x | | |
| | 7 | x | | |
| | 8 | x | | |
| **Dinos for Dinner** (pages 28–32) | 1 | x | | |
| | 2 | x | | |
| | 3 | | | x |
| | 4 | x | | |
| | 5 | | x | |
| | 6 | | x | |
| | 7 | x | | |
| | 8 | x | | |

# Question Types *(cont.)*

| Practice Exercise Title | Item | Key Ideas and Details | Craft and Structure | Integration of Knowledge and Ideas |
|---|---|---|---|---|
| A Royal Return to Russia (pages 33–37) | 1 | x | | |
| | 2 | | x | |
| | 3 | | x | |
| | 4 | | | x |
| | 5 | x | | |
| | 6 | x | | |
| | 7 | x | | |
| | 8 | x | | |
| These Robots are Wild (pages 38–42) | 1 | x | | |
| | 2 | x | | |
| | 3 | x | | |
| | 4 | | x | |
| | 5 | | | x |
| | 6 | | x | |
| | 7 | | | x |
| | 8 | x | | |
| Genghis Khan and the Mongol Empire (pages 43–47) | 1 | x | | |
| | 2 | | x | |
| | 3 | | x | |
| | 4 | x | | |
| | 5 | x | | |
| | 6 | | | x |
| | 7 | x | | |
| | 8 | x | | |
| Greening Africa (pages 48–51) | 1 | x | | |
| | 2 | x | | |
| | 3 | x | | |
| | 4 | | | x |
| | 5 | | x | |
| | 6 | | x | |
| | 7 | x | | |
| | 8 | x | | |
| The Newsies Strike (pages 52–56) | 1 | x | | |
| | 2 | | x | |
| | 3 | | | x |
| | 4 | x | | |
| | 5 | x | | |
| | 6 | | | x |
| | 7 | x | | |
| | 8 | x | | |

# Question Types *(cont.)*

| Practice Exercise Title | Item | Key Ideas and Details | Craft and Structure | Integration of Knowledge and Ideas |
|---|---|---|---|---|
| **It Takes One to Know One** (pages 57–61) | 1 | | x | |
| | 2 | x | | |
| | 3 | x | | |
| | 4 | x | | |
| | 5 | | x | |
| | 6 | | | x |
| | 7 | x | | |
| | 8 | | | x |
| **The Man Who Never Lied** (pages 62–66) | 1 | x | | |
| | 2 | | x | |
| | 3 | | x | |
| | 4 | x | | |
| | 5 | x | | |
| | 6 | | x | |
| | 7 | | | x |
| | 8 | x | | |
| **The Embarrassing Episode of Little Miss Muffett** (pages 67–70) | 1 | x | | |
| | 2 | | | x |
| | 3 | x | | |
| | 4 | | x | |
| | 5 | | x | |
| | 6 | | | x |
| | 7 | | x | |
| | 8 | | | x |
| **Barbara Frietchie** (pages 71–75) | 1 | x | | |
| | 2 | x | | |
| | 3 | x | | |
| | 4 | | x | |
| | 5 | | x | |
| | 6 | | x | |
| | 7 | x | | |
| | 8 | | | x |
| **Anglezandria and the Golden Tri-Scarab** (pages 76–81) | 1 | | x | |
| | 2 | | x | |
| | 3 | x | | |
| | 4 | x | | |
| | 5 | | | x |
| | 6 | | x | |
| | 7 | x | | |
| | 8 | x | | |

# Question Types (cont.)

| Practice Exercise Title | Item | Key Ideas and Details | Craft and Structure | Integration of Knowledge and Ideas |
|---|---|---|---|---|
| Women's Suffrage (pages 82–87) | 1 | x | | |
| | 2 | | x | |
| | 3 | | x | |
| | 4 | x | | |
| | 5 | x | | |
| | 6 | | | x |
| | 7 | x | | |
| | 8 | x | | |
| Arthur and the Pendragon Sword (pages 88–92) | 1 | x | | |
| | 2 | x | | |
| | 3 | x | | |
| | 4 | | x | |
| | 5 | | x | |
| | 6 | | | x |
| | 7 | x | | |
| | 8 | x | | |
| The Bees and the Beetle (pages 93–94) | 1 | | | x |
| | 2 | | x | |
| | 3 | x | | |
| Abuzz at a Hotel (pages 95–96) | 4 | x | | |
| | 5 | | x | |
| | 6 | | | x |
| The Bees and the Beetle and Abuzz at a Hotel (page 97) | 7 | | | x |
| | 8 | | | x |
| | 9 | | | x |
| Sympathy (pages 98–99) | 1 | | x | |
| | 2 | x | | |
| | 3 | | | x |
| She Never Stopped Fighting: Shirley Chisholm (pages 100–102) | 4 | | x | |
| | 5 | | | x |
| | 6 | x | | |
| Sympathy and She Never Stopped Fighting... (page 103) | 7 | | | x |
| | 8 | | | x |
| | 9 | | | x |

# Testing Tips

## Reading

**READ** more nonfiction texts with students!

## Writing

Encourage students to **SHOW** what they know with text-based **PROOF**!

## How Do I Help Students Prepare for Today's Tests?

## Mathematics

Help students **EXPLAIN** what's in their brains and **CONNECT** mathematics to the real world!

## Listening

**DISCUSS** what you read! **ANALYZE** what you think! **SYNTHESIZE** information!!

# Testing Tips *(cont.)*

| | | |
|---|---|---|
| Jail the Detail! | | Highlight, underline, or circle the details in the questions. This helps FOCUS on what the question is asking. |
| Be Slick and Predict! | | Predict what the answer is BEFORE you read the choices! |
| Slash the Trash! | | Read ALL the answer choices. "Trash" the choices that you know are incorrect. |
| Plug It In! Plug It In! | | Once you choose an answer, PLUG IT IN! Make sure your answer makes sense, especially with vocabulary and math. |
| Be Smart with Charts! Zap the Maps! | | Charts and maps provide information that you can use to answer some questions. Analyze ALL information before answering a question! |
| Extra! Extra! Read All About It! | | If the directions say read . . . READ! Pay close attention to signal words in the directions, such as *explain*, *interpret*, and *compare*. |
| If You Snooze, You Might Lose! | | Do not leave questions unanswered. Answering questions increases your chances of getting correct answers! |
| Check It Out! | | After you complete the test, go back and check your work! |

# Answer Key

**But What Did They Write About?** (pages 13–17)

1. A. The stone was discovered in Veracruz in 2006.

   B. The message on the slab was written around 1000 B.C.E.

2. D. "To most people, it may not even be clear that it *is* a message."

3. B. how complex the symbols are.

4. D. interpreted

5. E. "Historians have spent years trying to crack language codes . . . ."

6. C. It may hold the oldest form of writing ever found in the Americas.

7. Answers should include four of the following options in each column:

| What is KNOWN about the Mexican stone? | What is NOT KNOWN about the Mexican stone? |
|---|---|
| The stone has a message. The stone was written over 3,000 years ago, around 1000 B.C.E. The stone was found in Veracruz in 2006. There are 28 symbols. The symbols are scratches. The stone is 14 inches (35 cm). The symbols look like shapes. The language is similar to that of the Olmecs. | who wrote the message what the message says what the language is very much about the Olmecs who might decode it— amateurs or historians |

8. In 1900, a form of writing was found on the island of Crete in the Mediterranean Sea. More than a century later, no one knows what it says. The same thing may happen with the Mexican stone. It could be more than 100 years—if ever—before we know what it says.

**Peggy Whitson's Long Road to Space** (pages 18–22)

1. B. She saw the TV broadcast of Neil Armstrong and Buzz Aldrin on the moon.

   C. NASA sent two women into space when Whitson was in high school.

2. D. Whitson chose to keep pursuing her dream despite others' opinions.

3. A. "In 1996, she was admitted! It was her tenth try."

4. B. chance

5. G. Whitson's college was near NASA's Johnson Space Center.

6. A. It takes years of training to prepare for such a complicated job.

7. The timeline should include four of the following events and should be in chronological order.

| Year | Event Description |
|---|---|
| 1969 | Whitson watches Neil Armstrong and Buzz Aldrin walk on the moon on TV. |
| 1986 | Whitson gets a job at the Space Center. |
| 1996 | Whitson is admitted to NASA and becomes an astronaut. |
| 2002 | Whitson lives at the International Space Station for six months. |
| 2007 | Whitson goes back to the International Space Station. |
| 2009 | Whitson becomes the first female chief of NASA's Astronaut Office. |

8. Her time in space was worth the years of hard work. She worked long and hard to be an astronaut, and she said, "Leaving the Space Station was extremely difficult." She would not have said this if she didn't love what she did.

# Answer Key (cont.)

**Science and the Environment: Are They Enemies?**
(pages 23–27)

1. C. to show that the words come from Gaylord Nelson

2. B. extreme

3. E. "It was a time when people were acting out against their parents' way of life."

4. B. "Some adults thought Earth Day supporters had gone too far."

   D. "These adults made fun of the supporters, calling them 'tree huggers.'"

5. A. People are working together to solve fuel problems.

6. D. Science can be used to help protect the environment.

7. Answers should include four quotes from the text in each column.

| Earth Day in the 1970s | Earth Day Now |
|---|---|
| "But when it first started, Earth Day was seen as a radical protest." | "People realize that science and the environment do not have to be enemies." |
| "A lot of young people felt that science was the enemy even though some scientists were helpful." | "Technology can be used to protect the environment." |
| "Some scientists were warning the public about air and water pollution and animals in danger." | "It does not have to hurt it." |
| "Wasn't it technology—cars, housing developments, and factories—that was causing the problem?" | "Earth Day has grown up, and so has our view of science and nature." |
| "Wasn't it spreading pollution and destroying nature?" | "Now we know that we do not have to choose between the two because science can be used to protect the environment." |
| "Some adults thought Earth Day supporters had gone too far." | "You can be a scientist and a tree hugger." |
| "These adults made fun of the supporters, calling them 'tree huggers.'" | |
| "It was as if you had to choose: science or nature. You couldn't have both." | |

8. The statement means that our view of science and nature has matured. We no longer only think of them as being two individual focuses; rather, we know they can work together to benefit our world.

**Dinos for Dinner** (pages 28–32)

1. A. Farmers thought that the fossil might be important.

   B. Different scientists worked together to study the fossil.

2. C. "'This discovery is the chance of a lifetime,' Jin Meng says."

3. D. The dinosaur bones were found in the mammal's stomach.

4. A. a discovery changed scientists' thinking about mammals.

5. C. prehistoric

6. H. "Of course 130 million years ago, most dinosaurs were larger, stronger, and moved faster than mammals."

7. 3. Paleontologists found bones in the fossil's stomach.

   2. Farmers in China dug up a fossil and sent it to Bejing.

   5. Scientists discovered an animal called Repenomamus giganticus.

   1. A mammal ate a baby dinosaur in large chunks.

   4. Scientists realized that mammals were bigger than they thought.

8. The main idea is that new discoveries prompt new questions to be researched. "They [the new finds] leave you with more questions than answers."

**A Royal Return to Russia** (pages 33–37)

1. D. He was wealthy.

2. A. valued

3. H. "Russians celebrated the return of the treasures."

4. B. the egg is both exquisite and expensive.

5. B. They were skilled artisans.

6. C. "Fabergé eggs have long been the symbolic crown jewel of Russia's royal past."

7. Possible words include: wealthy, rich, generous, successful, thoughtful, and patriotic.

8. Any justified response is acceptable; potential responses include the following: Victor Vekselberg is wealthy and successful because he could afford to buy the eggs: "Vekselberg purchased the Fabergé eggs . . . worth an estimated $100 million." He is patriotic, thoughtful, and generous: "This was a once-in-a-lifetime chance to give back to my country one of its most revered treasures," he says. "I am honored to make this important collection available to the Russian public."

# Answer Key *(cont.)*

**These Robots Are Wild** (pages 38–42)

1. A. "They're fast. They're agile.

   C. "And they're easy to take care of."
2. D. insects, crustaceans, and arachnids
3. F. "They are able to travel quickly over rocky or uneven ground."
4. B. target
5. A. The robots imitate animal behaviors.
6. C. scientists think that lobsters have skills worth imitating.
7. Students may justify additional responses.

| Arthropod Skill | Environment Where It Would Be Useful |
|---|---|
| climbing | finding a person in a rockslide or avalanche, etc. |
| crawling | finding a person in a rockslide or avalanche, searching for someone lost in a cave, searching for survivors in rubble after a building collapses |
| swimming | searching for sunken ships, for new species of fish, for divers caught underwater |
| smelling | finding a gas leak, searching for drugs, blood, evidence from a fire |

8. This sentence summarizes the article: "By acting like bugs, these robots may help humans unlock the mysteries of the universe." It means that robots can explore areas that humans cannot reach or travel to because of our biological limitations.

**Genghis Khan and the Mongol Empire** (pages 43–47)

1. D. "He escaped slavery and lived as an outlaw."
2. D. dominate
3. A. They used what they learned about gunpowder to invent the cannon.
4. C. It shows that the Mongols had a tolerant side.
5. F. "The Mongols encouraged new ideas, new systems of writing, and scientific investigation."
6. B. the extent of the Mongols' control.
7. Accept any three in each column:

| Positive Influences | Negative Influences |
|---|---|
| There was freedom of religion. People earned their jobs through ability. The rulers encouraged new ideas. The rulers encouraged new systems of writing. The rulers encouraged scientific investigations. Art, culture, and learning traveled across the empire. | Their army struck fear into its opponents, using new tactics. They used siege warfare. They invented the cannon. They were ruthless in battle. |

8. By the time of the Black Plague, several generations had lived under the reign of the Khans. These generations had established "the great trading of ideas and cultures" that Genghis Khan promoted.

# Answer Key (cont.)

**Greening Africa** (pages 48–51)

1. B. "Across northern Africa, the desert is steadily growing."

2. D. Farmers are planting millions of crops and trees.

3. A. The project is made of growing things.

4. D. to show the location of the Great Green Wall

5. C. large-scale

6. G. "The Great Green Wall will eventually cover an area more than 4,000 miles (6,437 km) long."

7. Answers may indicate that the project is a success because people are sharing ideas, the wall is a cooperative effort that it will bring more jobs, and it will hold back the desert. Another possible answer is that the project is not yet a success because only two countries are discussed as being involved and it's not complete.

8. Answers should indicate that people are sharing ideas, they are working together, farmers are using water wisely, they are using the land wisely, crops are growing, the soil is richer, animals can graze, and the desert won't continue to spread.

**The Newsies Strike** (pages 52–56)

1. B. The adults don't want to be involved with the newsies.

2. C. strikebreaker

3. A. the clothing and ages of the newsies.

4. B. The newspaper seller relies on selling papers to survive.

5. H. "It was hard enough to make any dough when the papers cost a half-cent each."

6. D. to show that the boys are not well educated

7. Answers should include two of the following in each column.

| Jackie's Justifications for Selling Papers | Mike's Justifications for Supporting the Strike |
|---|---|
| He needs to make a living. | The newsies have to stick together to succeed. |
| He is poor. | The newsies have to fight back against the price increase. |
| | The newsies have to spread the word about the strike. |

8. Jackie is right because he relies on the little bit that he makes to eat. He is desperate. OR Mike is right because the newsies have to send a message to the newspapers that price increases are unacceptable. Mike is right because the newsies can accomplish more as a group working together.

**It Takes One to Know One** (pages 57–61)

1. C. questioning

2. B. to show how much Carl responds like a human

3. E. "Carl 562's face turned red."

4. D. Carl was programmed to speak with expression.

5. A. "Why don't you let us take out your memory chip . . . ."

6. B. The title explains how the narrator can think like Carl 562.

7. Answers will vary but may include the following:

| Setting Interrogation room | Time The future |
|---|---|
| **Characters** Sergeant Culligan, the narrator, Carl 562 | |
| **Problem** Carl 562 has stolen money. | |
| **Events** The narrator questions Carl. The narrator threatens to take out Carl's memory chip. | |
| **Resolution** Carl 562 confesses. The money is returned. Carl 562 is reprogramed as a gardener. | |

8. When the narrator states, "'Don't forget, Culligan,' I replied, 'that I am a J-class robot myself,'" the reader is surprised to learn that the narrator is not human. The way the narrator talks about Carl 562 has made the reader identify with him as a fellow human. For example, the narrator says, "Now that I was sitting just a few feet away, I could see that he was very realistic" and "I almost offered him a glass of water, but of course there was no point in that."

# Answer Key *(cont.)*

**The Man Who Never Lied** (pages 62–66)

1. D. A king was intrigued by a man who never tells lies.

2. A. aroused

3. A. It helps the reader to understand the king's attitude. C. It helps the reader to understand how Akili avoids lying.

4. B. cooperative
   C. humble

5. F. "'I can promise you that,' replied Akili, without a hint of vanity."

6. D. "Tomorrow, he will be proven a liar, and I will have an enormous laugh at his expense."

7. The author includes the line "Adapted from an African folktale" to give the reader an idea of the story's age and origin. Including this line lets the reader know that the story is so old and has been passed down by word of mouth. No one knows who first told it.

8. Answers should approximate the following:

| Event 1 | The king is interested in the man who never tells lies. |
|---------|---------------------------------------------------------|
| Event 2 | The king talks with Akili and makes him promise to never lie. |
| Event 3 | In an effort to trick Akili into lying, the king sends Akili to the queen with a message. |
| Event 4 | Akili tells the queen that the king may or may not arrive for the feast the next day. |
| Event 5 | When the queen reports what Akili tells her, the king learns that Akili is wise, only stating facts that he can verify. |

**The Embarrassing Episode of Little Miss Muffet** (pages 67–70)

1. B. Little Miss Muffet finds a place to have her lunch.

2. D. to support the rhyme and rhythm

3. A. "I'm penitent that I did not bring my hat."
   B. "Though anxious to please, he was so ill at ease"

4. C. incompetent

5. F. "This curious error completed her terror."

6. A. to define unfamiliar words

7. The answers should include one of the following in each column.

| See | Hear | Feel | Taste | Smell |
|-----|------|------|-------|-------|
| tuffet | rivulet | tuffet | whey | whey |
| rivulet | spider | spider | | |
| dragonflies | talking | (when she hit it) | | |
| spider | | | | |

8. The author plays with the word *whey*. There are three words in the English language that sound like whey (way and weigh). When the spider stepped into Miss Muffet's whey, he also got in her "way." So the author used wordplay, or verbal wit, to draw a parallel between whey and the saying "to get in the way" in order to make the reader chuckle.

# Answer Key *(cont.)*

**Barbara Frietchie** (pages 71–75)

1. A. "... bowed with her fourscore years and ten;"
2. C. that the townspeople had removed all the flags
3. A. "'Halt!'—the dust-brown ranks stood fast."
   B. "'Fire!'—out blazed the rifle-blast."
4. D. ripped
5. G. "Ever its torn folds rose and fell on the loyal winds that loved it well."
6. D. "'Shoot, if you must, this old gray head, but spare your country's flag,' she said."
7. Answers should indicate the following key events.

| Event 1 | Lee marches into Frederick. |
| Event 2 | The men of the town haul down the Union flag. |
| Event 3 | Barbara Frietchie places a Union flag in her attic window. |
| Event 4 | Rebels shoot at the flag in her window. |
| Event 5 | Barbara Frietchie shakes the flag, calling out to them to spare the flag. |
| Event 6 | Stonewall Jackson calls out to spare the flag and the woman. |

8. The author supports the Union cause. Possible lines to justify this include the following:

   "All day long that free flag tost over the heads of the rebel host; / Ever its torn folds rose and fell on the loyal winds that loved it well."

   "And through the hill-gaps sunset light shone over it with a warm good night. / Now Barbara Frietchie's work is o'er and the Rebel rides on raids no more."

   "Peace and order and beauty draw / 'Round thy symbol of light and law;"

**Anglezandria and the Golden Tri-Scarab**
(pages 76–81)

1. A. cherishes
2. H. "My successor must be someone who loves math and this great city as much as I do."
3. B. He holds great power and likes math.
4. A. "It's their teamwork that puts them ahead of the others."
   D. "The two help each other, which is why they can quickly solve the riddles."
5. C. describe the actions of characters.
6. B. Those names fit with the theme of solving math puzzles.
7. Possible answers include:

   Acutus and Pentagonus circle: They work together to solve the riddles. They are intelligent.

   Intersection of circles: They are Anglezandrians. They are competing to be the next pharoah.

   Other Anglezandrians circle: They are lost and confused. They chose to work alone.

8. Acutus is very knowledgeable with math and is able to draw shapes for Pentagonus. Since Pentagonus knows the city so well, he is able to look at Acutus's drawings and identify the landmarks that hold the next clues. They both utilize each other's strengths.

# Answer Key *(cont.)*

**Women's Suffrage** (pages 82–87)

1. D. "We need to continue our work to change each state's constitution, state by state."

2. B. strategies

3. C. "We have decided that we must hold a huge suffrage parade in Washington . . . ."

4. B. "I believe it is up to each state to decide whether women should vote."

5. G. "I'm quite sure that this issue will die over the next four years."

   H. "Passing an amendment to the Constitution is very, very difficult."

6. A. The drama makes the reader feel as if he or she is part of the action.

7. Possible answers include:

   Carrie Catt circle: wants to work on the cause state by state; doesn't listen to others; doesn't achieve her goal

   Intersection of circles: both are a part of NAWSA; both want women's rights

   Alice Paul circle: wants to take more extreme measures; listens to others; achieves her goal

8. Alice Paul is successful because she doesn't take no for an answer. She knows what needs to be done to achieve her goal. To achieve her goal, she leaves NAWSA and starts a new organization, she leads the women's suffrage parade, and she gets Woodrow Wilson to listen to her.

**Arthur and The Pendragon Sword** (pages 88–92)

1. B. " . . .Merlin convinced Uther to relinquish the newborn for safekeeping."

2. C. He is devoted to Uther Pendragon.

3. A. "Within a year, King Uther and his wife lay dead from a traitor's poison . . . "

4. B. disorder

5. E. " . . . Britain endured violence and chaos as kings, dukes, and lords fought for control."

6. D. summarize the action over time.

7. Possible answers include: dedicated, loyal, kind, trustworthy, or patient.

8. Since Merlin foresees the untimely death of Uther Pendragon and Lady Igraine, everyone works out a plan to keep the newborn child safe until he can become the rightful king. Had Merlin not done this, the newborn would never have made it to his 18th birthday, and he would never have had the opportunity to become the king.

**The Bees and the Beetle** (pages 93–94)

1. D. The animals talk like humans, and the story teaches a lesson.

2. B. the beetle tells the bees to create a new honeycomb.

3. C. One's actions speak louder than one's words.

**Abuzz at a Hotel** (pages 95–96)

4. D. having a beehive at a hotel is beneficial.

5. B. They help the reader to understand the importance of the bees.

   D. They help the reader to understand how the honey is used.

6. A. "The beehives share the rooftop with a garden."

**The Bees and the Beetle and Abuzz at a Hotel** (page 97)

7. A. The main idea of the fable is the moral about work; the main idea of the article is the contribution of the bees at a hotel.

8. B. work hard to make honey.

   C. are valued for their honey.

9. D. teach a moral and describe an unusual place for a beehive.

**Sympathy** (pages 98–99)

1. B. branch

2. D. "It is not a carol of joy or glee, / But a prayer that he sends from his heart's deep core,"

3. B. stanzas

   C. rhyming

**She Never Stopped Fighting: Shirley Chisholm** (pages 100–102)

4. A. strength

5. D. to organize the article by topic

6. B. She devoted her life to fighting for others.

**Sympathy and She Never Stopped Fighting: Shirley Chisholm** (page 103)

7. A. "I ran for the presidency, despite hopeless odds."
   C. "She was never afraid to speak out."

8. B. "For he must fly back to his perch and cling"

9. D. fighting against the odds.

# Notes

# Notes

# Notes